Kalami

Where the Sea Shrugs its Shoulders

By

D.J. Smithers

Copyright DJ Smithers © 2012

All rights reserved. No part of this book may be reproduced in any form, except for the inclusion of brief quotations in reviews, without the written permission from the author.

All events and characters depicted in this book are real but some of the names where appropriate have been changed.

2nd Edition reprinted 2015

Dedication

This book is dedicated to my dear wife, Julie, without whom the holidays in Kalami, and my life, would be only half as enjoyable. Also, to all the friends we've made during our visits there and to the many friends we've yet to meet for we cannot envisage a time when we will ever stop our sojourns to this idyll. It is also dedicated to the wonderful people of Corfu and especially to Thomas and Alexandra whose friendship and hospitality draw us back time and time again.

www.davidjohn37.co.uk

Preface

I had many reservations about writing this book. Namely that after finding this piece of nirvana my wife & I wanted to keep it to ourselves. We didn't want the rest of the world to know about it. But then I realised I was being a bit presumptuous, thinking that thousands of people were going to read this book and go running off to invade this little bit of paradise. Hopefully, though, it may inspire some to want to experience the beauty and sereneness of this small corner of Corfu.

This is not a romantic novel, although falling in love with a place could be classed as romantic I suppose. It's not a travelogue either for it is not broad enough to qualify as that. It's not even an attempt at history or ethnicity of the Corfiot people or even Kalami itself for detail is very scant. It is a book that has taken me eight years to write though.

What it is is a collection of events and anecdotes, many humorous, that we have witnessed over the handful of years that we have returned time and time again to this wonderful place. It is also about an assortment of people; some interesting; some enthralling; some strange; most eccentric. All of the events that happened in this book actually took place but to save embarrassment (and possible liable action!), some of the names have been changed. I've tried to describe not just what we saw but what we felt. It's hard to put into words the feeling of a place; you just have to go there to experience it yourself. Hopefully, this book will inspire you to do just that.

Kalami

Where the Sea Shrugs its Shoulders

Chapter 1

Research

"I took my younger sister and my mum with me last year and we didn't like it at all. It was too steep and there were no nightclubs or discos! It was too quiet and boring". So wrote 19-year-old Katie from Sussex, awarding it just 5/10.

"Well, it's certainly got good reviews on the forums dear!" I remarked to Julie as she busied herself in the kitchen.

"You shouldn't go by those," she replied, "One man's meat and all that!"

"I know," I said, "but out of all of the reviews this is the only negative one, and it's a teenager saying that it was all too quiet. So it's gonna be perfect for us!"

I was busy on the net checking out a recommendation for our next two-week holiday. As was my wont, and to the annoyance of Julie, I always perused the holiday forum sites and read the reviews of travelled hardened vacationers for fear of ending up in the holiday from hell. You know the one. The one that's espoused so earnestly by the travel company, extolling the virtues of the:- hotel/apartments/villa; scenery/location/amenities; staff/locals/population; facilities/pastimes/sports; food/drink/entertainment, etc. Whereas, those that have stayed (or suffered) fill you in on all the little details like:- doss-house/fleapit/brothel; remote/desolate/isolated; rude/aggressive/scary; boring/broken/dull; under-cooked/over-priced/over-stated!

    For example, one holiday in Greece was described by the travel company of having *'Outstandingly beautiful views across the bay from the apartment balcony.'* On the forum, guests had agreed that the views across the bay were indeed outstandingly beautiful. But, what the brochure had omitted to mention was also the view across the main road passing just outside the apartment block that ran continuously 24 hours a day! Or another that had waxed lyrical about the *'.....small Spanish family-run hotel that felt like home from home!'* However, the reality was that they were more like the Mafia family, demanding payments for anything and everything while delivering little, and then having the cheek to leave a 'tips' tin in your room on your day of departure!

    The views and narratives I found of Kalami Bay, Corfu, were just as described to us by a mutual friend. Charming, peaceful, small, friendly and above all, secluded. Julie and I had been together for a couple of years now and, as singletons, had both travelled to different places. I hadn't started venturing abroad until after I got divorced from my first wife, so I was pushing 40 before I stepped out into the big, wide world of continental travel. Unfortunately, by the time I met Julie, my somewhat limited jet-setting consisted of just Malta, Gran Canaria and Crete. Whereas Julie was slightly more travelled, having visited Norway, Switzerland, Belgium, France, Germany, Holland, Andorra, Fuerteventura, and a fair chunk of America as she'd lived in California for ten years. But now we were together we were looking for somewhere we could call ours, our own little haven where we could return to on a regular basis. A place where we could feel at home and at peace. And so, on the strength of our friends say so and on the glut of positive feedback on a number of forums, we not only booked two weeks in Kalami in June but also booked another week in September, before we had even been out there! Such was our belief, or hope, that we had found our Nirvana.

We trawled endless websites thereafter, looking for more and more photos of our little paradise till we knew it better than our own town. It was small, with one road leading into it but not out, and with very little traffic except that of locals and delivery vans. There were about a dozen private villas, each more beautiful than the last, and one main apartment block, which would be our home for the time we were there. This was a cascade of brightly coloured blocks of apartments built into the steep hillside, affording breathtaking views from every floor across the bay which was lined on either side by Cypress and Olive trees and filled with the blue Ionian Sea stretching out towards Albania a few miles distant. Three tavernas lay along the beach spaced far apart like estranged brothers who no longer speak but are still watchful of each other. There was one small jetty where a gaily-coloured fishing boat was tied. The beach was pebbly. There were a couple of small bars and the inevitable mini-supermarkets. But above all, there were no nightclubs, no discos, no theme bars, no 18-hour a day sports bars, no water parks, no amusement arcades and no noise after midnight. Bliss! My kids had always called me a boring old fart, well, now I could fulfil that role to my heart's content!!!

We had many weeks to go before the holiday and I took pleasure in annoying the hell out of Julie by texting her each day with a countdown of how many were left. I eventually became fed up with this myself as it seemed like a lifetime to go before the holiday so I took to just texting her weekly instead. I knew our plane took off from Stansted at 8.20am on a Tuesday morning and I was fortunate that my job as a maintenance operative (a fancy term for a handyman), at a private college afforded me the opportunity to observe the comings and goings of the planes at the airport from a distance. I was also fortunate that for the three months leading up to the holiday I was decorating the top floor dormitories which were facing in the direction of Stansted. So every Tuesday morning, regular as clockwork, I would stand at the window and watch the 8.20 to Corfu emerge from behind the distant tree line and climb to its allotted flight path on its journey to warmer climes. I would then text Julie to say 'I've just seen our plane take off'. Where back would come the reply 'You're so sad!'

I also tried to find any Greek language courses we could enrol on so that we could learn the lingo before we got there but to no avail. By this time I was also starting to look at properties on the island, so convinced was I that we probably wouldn't want to come back. That England would end up our second home and Corfu our first. I do have a problem with going overboard with new ventures. Luckily Julie keeps me grounded.

Eventually, the weeks became days and the days hours until we found ourselves deposited at the airport at five in the morning. It was fortunate that Julie's daughter, Becki, worked for Swissport at the time and was on the early morning shift. It meant getting there well ahead of time but it saved on a taxi fare and we, like two little kids on their first ever trip abroad, couldn't wait to get in the holiday mood as soon as possible, which for us meant it started the moment we knocked off work the day before! We were the first in the queue with our tickets, first through the security checks and after a quick walk around the shops, breakfast and a few coffees we were the first out to the boarding gate even before they announced its opening. Unfortunately, we were the last to board as Julie suffers from bad nerves when having to wait on a plane. This came about after being stuck for over four hours with two toddlers on a plane at LAX after the luggage had to be removed and repacked when it emerged someone had left a lighter in their suitcase. Nobody was allowed off the aircraft and since then she has to make sure she visits the toilet umpteen times and at the very last minute before they close the gate. We could feel the eyes burning into us as we walked down the aisle to our seats. We could read the thoughts as they emanated from either side and then fired at us like mental arrows in the hope of inflicting some pain for delaying their holiday by a few minutes. 'Who do they think they are, walking on after everybody's sat down and strapped in? Think they own the bloody airline!' I knew what they were thinking and I wanted to shout "It's not me, it's her! I wanted to get on first but she had to do 84 toilet runs!" But I couldn't. Decorum forbade it and Julie would have killed me.

Eventually, the engines whined into life, the captain made the usual greetings and introductions and the cabin crew did their safety rounds making sure we were all securely strapped in. Then the jolt as we were shunted backwards out onto the tarmac followed by the inevitable wait for clearance before we began our taxi. You could feel the apprehension mounting as we inched slowly forward to our holding position. Not because of flying nerves or because the cabin crew were going through their 'best position to be in just before you die' routine, but you were never sure whether you were going to be called back any second and delayed for hours due to some technical fault or ATC strike or baggage handlers go-slow or dead pilot on board. Fortunately, none of these occurred and we nosed forward on to the main runway, sank back in our seats as the engines throttled up, rumbled down the noisy, uneven tarmac, pointed skywards and became that 8.20 Tuesday flight to Corfu.

Chapter 2

Paradise?

The approach to Corfu airport was at first overwhelming. We flew just a few hundred feet above the sea, flanked by Albania on our left and the eastern coastline of Corfu to our right. The hot Mediterranean sun poured in through the windows and far below glinted and shimmered off the mirrored waters. We recited the names of every cove and bay as we headed south, having memorised them from the countless books and websites we'd perused. Kassiopi; Agios Stefanos; Kouloura; Kalami; Agni; Nisaki; Barbati; Ypsos; Gouvia; until we banked sharply right and headed over Corfu port and circled round to begin our descent to the runway. At this point the breathtaking views, shimmering waters, beautiful bays and rugged coastline went by-the-by as we suddenly realised that not only did we have to try and touch down without ditching in the said shimmering waters, but that we seemed to still be flying at 500 miles an hour and that once down we had what appeared to be about the length of a cricket pitch in which to stop! There were yachts below us which had tyre marks on their sails and the crews were wearing hard hats! We gripped the armrests, we gripped each other, Julie even gripped the person next to her but they were too busy praying to notice! The sea and the runway were both rushing up to meet us at a rate of knots but which one we'd reach first only the pilot and God knew, and we weren't overly confident about the pilot!

Finally, the wheels made contact with the tarmac with that heart-stopping but at the same time reassuring squeal of rubber. Convinced that we were still going too fast both Julie and I tried an emergency stop using the imaginary brake pedal that we had on the floor in front of us, but to no avail. Looking around it seems the other 300 other passengers had one as well but none of theirs seemed to be working either! Fortunately, the pilot decided to use his and we suddenly found ourselves being accelerated forward in our seats at about 100mph, the problem being that the plane now was only doing about 50mph! The effect of this was to cause the seatbelt, which only goes around your middle, to suddenly try to become part of your intestines. This is obviously why the meals on planes are kept to a minimum, to save the crew having to clear up a regurgitated breakfast travelling at something close to the speed of light. Fortunately, most people had used the toilet facilities during flight so this helped keep other bodily fluids from being expelled.

We finally came to rest in the unloading area where everybody gave a sigh of relief, packed their prayer beads away and, in the British time-honoured fashion of good manners and patience, poured out of their seats and scrambled to recover their hand luggage from the overhead racks before charging down the aisle to be first off the plane in case the sun suddenly went out. The elderly and infirm stood no chance if they tried to leave their seats during this melee. Likewise, the stewards and stewardesses, being highly professional and well seasoned, got the hell out of the way and cowered in the corner.

As we stepped out of the pressurised tube that had been our home for the past three hours we were instantly enshrouded by the heat. It wasn't a sticky or unpleasant heat; it was a heat that instantly cleared your mind of any thoughts of the chilly, damp country we had left behind. It was a heat that welcomed you with open arms but asked for nothing in return. It was a heat that you felt permeated every muscle, every sinew, every ounce of flesh until, like a warm electric blanket, you sunk lower and lower into its solace.

Once off we were all herded onto the transfer buses where we sat for nearly ten minutes before the driver was given the all clear to drive round the other side of the plane and deposit us at the arrivals ramp. On foot, this would have taken us less than 30 seconds to achieve? Safely delivered we tramped up the ramp to be met by a bored looking official sitting in a kiosk who just nodded here and there as we streamed by either side, dutifully displaying our passports like good little tourists. Personally, he couldn't give a damn if we were tourists or terrorists, as long as he could get out of that square, stifling goldfish bowl ASAP.

Once through it was the customary charge to the baggage area where we tried to guess which carousel ours would emerge from. Everybody was crowding round the only vacant belt, all jostling for that all important space near the opening in the hope of getting their luggage first. We all stood expectantly and excitedly, waiting for the first glimpse of a suitcase or travel bag or holdall, hoping that nobody else had the same luggage as us. This was normally cured by buying the gaudiest coloured baggage you could find knowing that nobody else would be daft enough to do the same, but then backing out at the last minute as you didn't want to be the one with the gaudiest coloured baggage you could find.

Suddenly, the conveyor belt juddered into motion and there was a swift surge forward, each of us staring transfixed and ready, hoping to be the first away with their bags. The minutes passed and the air became thick with tension. Sweaty brows joined sweaty palms, feet started to fidget, eyes were glued fixedly to that one magical, mysterious aperture from whence, any moment, your luggage would emerge and you would grab it triumphantly and stroll smugly through the now despondent throng, baggage in tow, head held high, knowing you're the first on the coach.

It was becoming unbearable. Furtive and untrusting glances were bouncing around the room. Shoulders and stances were widened so that personal spaces couldn't be encroached upon. Brows furrowed and a deathly hush fell on the throng. Waiting! Waiting! Waiting! There were a few nonchalant ones, those that had been here before and knew the score. They stood there blasé, hands in pockets or arms folded, looking at their feet, or out the window, or at their nails, or with backs turned as if they couldn't care less when their luggage would emerge. They were used to the Greek way of doing things, which was akin to the Spanish mañana, 'tomorrow'. So to them, it came when it came. But to the rest of us, there was the fear. Had they lost the entire luggage and it was now en route to Birmingham? Is the coach gonna go without us because we took too long to get our bags?? Has there been a baggage handlers strike the moment we touched down and we won't be seeing our luggage until the day we fly back??? All this just increased the tension to unbearable limits. If we came here to chill out it wasn't a very good start.

> Suddenly a voice went up.
> "Over here, this is our belt!"

As one body we all turned to see our baggage emerging from the other carousel behind us and as one conjoined animal, we surged forward, intent on taking up our corresponding places around the other belt. Those that had been at the front of the throng were now cast to the back in the move as those that had been at the back got to the other belt first. Having had their noses put out of joint at losing their front row status many a jostling was taking place as the Alpha male and female tried to reassert their position. In their haste many a wrong suitcase was mistakenly picked up, name tag read and re-deposited unceremoniously back onto the belt. Some struggled to lift theirs off the carousel quick enough which resulted in them chasing their luggage along the belt, colliding with all and sundry that made up the front row causing them to, begrudgingly but hastily, take a step back quickly stepping forward again for fear of losing their place to some interloper. With those standing behind being so close, they also had to take a step back and forward. This gave the effect of a Mexican wave, but in a lateral rather than vertical direction.

It's a strange phenomenon but why is it that every airport you go to the first piece of luggage to emerge is never claimed by anybody and just sits there going round and round?

Our luggage finally retrieved we found our rep, was directed to our bus and boarded in the hope that we would soon be on our way to Kalami. Thirty minutes later found us still sitting on the bus waiting for late arrivals and melting in the heat as there was no air-conditioning unless the engine was running. Obviously, the driver, being Greek, wasn't affected by the heat and didn't think the air-con was needed. Either that or he just hated tourists? Five minutes later the last of the passengers were onboard and we were off, following the road that skirted the airport before heading off into the busy main drag of Corfu town. Here streets became narrow and winding, sometimes only just wide enough for a car to squeeze through between the rows of parked vehicles hugging the kerbs, but somehow we managed to negotiate a full-size coach up these roads without so much as a scratch or a scrape. Traffic seemed to come from every direction; every turning; every side street; and all force themselves in front of our bus. The streets were thronging with tourists and locals, although sometimes it was hard to tell the difference as everybody sported a bronzed tan. The only way you could tell them apart was that the tourists liked to show theirs off with sleeveless tops, unbuttoned shirts, short trousers and occasional bare torsos.

Motorists parked anywhere and everywhere. Across pavements; two abreast; in no parking zones; middle of the road! Scores of motorcycles and scooters straddled by riders and passengers alike, all without helmets or leathers, most just wearing tee-shirts, shorts or miniskirts, weaved and dodged through any space they could find, most times on the wrong side of the road and often against the flow of traffic. But nobody seemed to care. There was no blasting of horns, no raised voices, no one or two fingered gestures, no swearing or threats. It was all an accepted part of Greek life. Little heed was paid to personal safety. It was as if they all drove with one mind and everybody knew what everybody else was going to do. Even our coach driver negotiated tight corners, suicidal bikers, maniacal truckers, speeding taxis and headstrong pedestrians all with one hand on the steering wheel while at the same time conducting a rather lengthy animated and sometimes heated conversation on his mobile phone. We had come to Corfu in the hope of finding our little paradise. It wasn't boding well.

Safely out of the centre of the town we followed the main dual carriageway north. To our right, numerous liners and ferries docked side by side in the port, loading and unloading passengers and vehicles alike. Some were local ferries that just nipped over to Albania or mainland Greece. Others went further afield like Turkey, Italy and to the countless other Greek islands. The liners were a mass of multi-floored, glass and steel gargantuans, towering above the dockside, full of their own majesty and importance. Enticing names like Splendour of the Seas, La Belle de L'Adriatiques, and our very own Queen Victoria challenged you not to be tempted to at least come and have a look round these seaborne palaces of luxury and opulence.

The broad ribbon of road climbed steadily as it left the near flatness of the urban sprawls and continued northward towards the rockier, volcanic landscape at the top of the island. To our left, every inch of steep hillside was planted with olive groves.

Beneath could be found the black nets, rolled and tied, awaiting that year's harvesting. Stone walls held back the earth, reaching higher than the roof of the coach in places. At each town, we deposited various computations of passengers. Two here; six there; the odd singles along the way. Eventually, we found ourselves following the picturesque coastal road overlooking bay after bay of whitewashed villas and blue waters.

Because of his somewhat lackadaisical approach to road safety and the fact his phone was continually glued to his ear, the coach found itself being driven, not by one careless Greek driver, but by 52 petrified tourists. Every hairpin bend and blind corner saw the entire entourage lean at 45 degrees like an Isle of Man TT rider, while at the same time stamping down on the imaginary brake pedal loaned from the aeroplane. A collective, audible sigh of relief could be heard when we negotiated the bends without hitting something head-on or disappearing over the cliff edge. Health and safety had not visited Corfu bus drivers!

Our destination was nearly upon us! As we rounded a right-hand bend the tops of the Adonis & Asonitis apartments, affectionately known as the Pink Palace, greeted us a few hundred yards up ahead. We could only see the uppermost floor as the others clung to the steep side of the cliffs while descending in stages towards the bay below. We were deposited at the top of the steps that wound down to our floor while other guests were taken by minibus down a steep road to the lower floors. We raced along the balcony dragging our suitcases behind us, the wheels click, click, clicking a rhythmical beat as they rolled across the ceramic-tiled balconies. We located our apartment that would be our home for the next two weeks, flung open the door, tossed our luggage onto the bed and threw open the green slatted doors that led to our balcony to be greeted by an incredible breathtaking view that swept down across the red clay tiled roofs to the bay and beyond. We stood there immersed in the beauty of the vista, the heat of the Mediterranean sun and the peppery aroma of the evergreen cypress. To our right, across the top of the headland which served to half enclose our little bay, could be seen the shimmering heat haze of Corfu town. In front was the steep coastline and the sesame seed bun landscape of Albania. And to the left the small headland that completed the bay and which encompassed pretty white and yellow Grecian villas draped in pink, apricot and crimson bougainvillaea surrounded by cypress and olive trees all which swept down to meet the calm, blue, warm Ionian waters.

    We heard nothing but our own breathing.

Within moments we had donned our costumes under our skimpy clothing and began to negotiate the meandering and sometimes confusing flights of stairs that led from our floor down to the reception area of the apartments, across the small road, through a rough car-park and then down onto the pebbly shore. This was a crescent-shaped beach that ran the length of the village, some fifty feet deep at our end tapering down a few feet at the other. A timber walkway lay unsteadily on the pebbles and stretched the length of the beach to facilitate ease of passage while at the same time giving easy access to the three tavernas that sat lazily and invitingly upon the top of the shoreline. Dark blue loungers with blue & white striped parasols were dotted sporadically along the water's edge draped with a mixture of bronzed bodies (been here two weeks), and white cadavers (been here two days). Within moments we had occupied two of them in front of the middle taverna, discarded everything but our costumes and were immediately transformed into two lily-white sun-worshipers hoping to be tanned to perfection by the end of the day. Unfortunately, the end of the day, sun-bathing wise, was only four hours away so our attempts to blend in with the locals after day one were overly optimistic, to say the least.

The mid-afternoon sun was begrudgingly opposed with copious amounts of factor 20 sunblock; dehydration abated with long, cold drinks from the taverna and overheating cooled by frequent swims in the clear waters. When standing still fish of all shapes, sizes and colours swam close by. The more brazen ones, normally the smaller fish, would venture close to your legs while the larger, timid ones would stay at a distance where they could disappear into the dark green haven of the seaweed that clung to the shingly bed at the first sign of danger. A brace of beautiful and highly expensive Sunseeker yachts were moored in the bay while their owners were either lunching at one of the tavernas or sunning themselves on the foredeck. Occasionally a ferry would pass on its way to Albania or Italy and the odd catamaran could be seen sailing along the coastline. A warm but gentle breeze subtly scented with the woody, spicy aroma of cypress, occasionally aided our cooling. Nothing could be heard except the gentle rolling of the waves on the pebbles, the occasional swimmer as they gambolled in the sea and the chug-chug-chugging of the brightly coloured fishing boat that ventured out periodically in search of dinner. All was definitely at peace with the world.

Kalami

Reluctantly we dragged ourselves away from this nirvana and by 7.30pm we had returned to our apartment, showered, changed and made our way back down to the taverna at the head of the beach. We chose a table as near to the front as possible so as to soak in the smells and sounds of the ocean as it broke on the shore. The taverna itself was a long affair, enclosed along the two sides with plastic walls, which gave it the appearance of a marquee. The front was rolled up exposing the inhabitants to the humid evening air and the cooling breeze that wafted across the water. We were both fairly adventurous gastronomy wise, Julie more so than me. I would eat most conventional meat dishes but drew the line at fish unless it was in batter. Julie, on the other hand, relished fares such as snails, mussels, squid, anything vegetarian and every fish imaginable. But we had both decided from the outset that we going to try and eat native as much as possible, the food that is, not the people. So with this in mind, we perused the offered menu and opened proceedings with sardines filled with cheese, mushrooms in garlic and a Greek salad. I followed this with Kleftico, a lamb dish I had so been looking forward to since trying it at an authentic Greek taverna in a village not too far from where we lived. Unfortunately, it didn't live up to expectations. Julie chose the chicken Souvlaki; grilled small pieces of meat and vegetables on a skewer, not unlike a Kebab. She found this too dry and tough for her liking. We downed everything with copious amounts of red and white wine and decided that the following night we'd opt for the next taverna in the hope of faring better.

When we finally dragged ourselves away from the wine the sun had set behind Mount Pantokrator, Corfu's highest mountain. The evening was still very warm so we traversed the beach towards the little jetty where the sea taxis docked to pick up and deposit those that wanted to experience Greek cuisine round at the next bay. We cut up between a couple of private dwellings to meet the road and headed back to our apartments, passing between a mixture of local houses and holiday villas. We climbed up the steep steps that a few hours before we had hurried down in the excited hope of a Grecian feast. We sat on our balcony drinking wine and looking out at the shimmering lights of Corfu town some 28kms distant. The sea was dark, only lit here and there by distant pin-pricks of light on the Albanian mainland. Occasionally the sea taxis would return to deposit sated diners and collect others yet to be fulfilled. They could be heard long before they were seen as onboard stereo systems blared out hits from ABBA and a throng of voices could be heard echoing Waterloo, Mama Mia and Voulez Vous. Initially, we wondered where this music emanated from as all that could be seen in the inky blackness was the red and green navigation lights of the boats as they rounded the headland, but as they neared so the music increased.

The day eventually caught up with us and we fell asleep to the sounds of the sea and the chirping of the cicadas. Our first day in Corfu hadn't boded well, but with all its quirky charm, I think we may have found our paradise?

Chapter 3

Cats and Cowboys

The rhythmic toll of nearby church bells brought us gently round from our slumbers, the faithful being summoned to worship. I rose and stepped out on to the balcony to be met by an early morning sunrise that already boasted of the heat yet to come. Below, early morning wares were being delivered to supermarkets and tavernas. Newspapers were dropped off at the gift shop: Greek broadsheets, as it was too early for the foreign journals. A lone cleaner sang quietly as she readied herself for the day. A taverna waiter, put-puting his way along the road on a moped far too small for him, arrived for work. The brightly coloured fishing boat returned to harbour with last night's catch. Kalami was waking up.

I tend to be a rather private person on holiday, preferring much my own company. But Julie is more of a sociable animal and will talk to anybody and everybody given the chance. Which is why, on the morning of the second day, I suddenly became aware of the fact that she had gone for a swim and not returned for a good 15 minutes. This was unusual because Julie was not one for staying in the water long; a quick dip to cool off, making sure she didn't get her hair wet, and then back to sunbathing. I turned over onto my back to see where she had got to only to find her standing just offshore in amongst two other couples, deep in conversation like long lost friends. I sighed and then turned back over before she spotted me and beckoned me over to join in. I'm not an unsociable creature but I'm always the one who befriends strangers only to have them turn out to be boring or over-bearing or loud or self-opinionated or sometimes psychotic! Julie's predilection for talking to all and sundry comes from her time spent as a care worker, tending for the elderly and infirm. She took the job too much to heart, so much so that she got herself into trouble one year when she felt so sorry for one little old lady that she collected her on Christmas morning and brought her home for dinner so she wouldn't be on her own!

"Dave!" "Dave!"

I tried to ignore the call as long as possible hoping that she would assume I was asleep. It didn't work.

"DAVE!!"

I eventually sat up to be met by Julie frantically beckoning me down to meet her new found friends. Begrudgingly I dragged myself away from the comfort of my lounger and waded in where I was introduced to Ian & Lesley and Pete & Jeanne. Hello's and pleasantries were exchanged while we all stood waist deep in the cooling waters. Eventually, conversation got round to occupations. I myself was working as a maintenance operative at a 300-year-old private college. A job, which I thought, would generate some interest for the historical aspect if nothing else. This was overshadowed by the fact that Ian was a sergeant in the Buckinghamshire police force, and Peter, who was well into his 60's, was a retired airline pilot with a penchant for windsurfing. And, the weirdest thing of all, that Peter had actually once worked with Julie's ex-husband at Macdonald-Douglass in California! How spooky is that!

Ian tended to hold centre stage, regaling many stories of incidents and anecdotes of his time in the force. These were met with a mixture of wonder, humour, disgust, astonishment, disbelief and envy. The stories were endless and continual, but never boring. He knew how to recount each tale with just the right amount of suspense or embellishment to keep his audience enthralled. Well, me anyway! Peter stood there somewhat indifferent to it all, but then he had probably heard these stories time and time again as he and Jeanne had been coming to Kalami for the past 25 years, and Ian & Lesley for 20. So for them, these stories weren't new – but the audience always was.

We had been standing in the water for so long that my lower half had lost all sense of feeling, while my top half had gone red from UV exposure. When I eventually emerged from the sea I looked like a vanilla and strawberry ice-lolly! While I retired to my lounger, Ian stayed in for a swim and Peter took to his windsurfer, this left the women to carry on chatting like three long lost sisters. I opened the parasol that accompanied my lounger so as to protect my glowing torso from the relentless sun and to give my white wrinkly legs a chance to catch up.

I lay with my eyes closed as the waves gently lapped and licked the shore in front of me, the sun burned hot above me and melodious Greek music played softly in the taverna behind.

That evening, through Ian's recommendation, saw us dining at Thomas's, a slightly smaller affair than the first night's taverna but considerably more convivial and run by a husband and wife team, Thomas and Alexandra. She greeted us with a huge but nervous smile, a result of the fact that she understood very little English and spoke even less. Thomas's demeanour was as warm as his greeting.

"Kalispera. How are you today?" he would ask earnestly.

He was soft spoken and with a better command of English than his wife. I later learned that not only did he run the taverna in the evenings and weekends but also drove to Corfu town five days a week to manage a business there. His day started around six each morning and didn't finish till after the last guest had bid goodnight, which could sometimes be around 1 am.

Everything from the atmosphere to the food was as near to perfect as you could get. You weren't just made to feel welcome; you were made to feel like one of the family. It was the epitome of Greek hospitality. Again, like the first time, we chose a table at the front of the taverna that had unobstructed views from one end of the beach to the other and straight out across the darkening waters. All very Shirley Valentine.

Choosing the table and wine were the easiest of options, half a carafe of red for me and white for Julie. Choosing what to eat however was more of a struggle? There were a myriad of starters followed by a multitude of main courses. These included Lamb hot-pot, Souvlaki, Yemista, Dolmades, Saganaki, Skordalia, Gigantes, Keftedes, Moussaka, Pastitsio, Stifado etc. Not to mention the countless fish dishes that Thomas was well known for. So-much-so that when the famous TV chef, Rick Stein, visited Corfu he made a point of dining at Thomas's to sample one of his fish delights. Unfortunately for me, they didn't serve Kleftico, so I opted for the lamb hotpot served with a cheese topping. They also did a starter to die for called Tiropitakia. These were small triangular cheese pies made with filo pastry and filled with Feta and Gouda or Parmesan. I blamed this cheese fest for my half stone increase in my weight while we were there – nothing to do with copious amounts of wine of course!

One of the unfortunate drawbacks of being well known for your fish cuisine is being well known for your fish cuisine by the local cat population. Cats are not treated as pets like they are in most countries, they are seen more as an unwelcome pest, and so, all are wild. At Thomas's, they are tolerated as they help to keep the vermin population in check and each night they could be found wandering between legs, both human and table, in the hope of a few scraps of dropped food. Some were kittens only a few weeks old, others were shabby and gaunt with age, but all would congregate around your chairs and stare at you with pleading eyes. No sound would emerge. No pitying cries were uttered. No mournful purrs whined. They just sat like porcelain figurines waiting until you could bear it no longer and spared them a little of your meal. If it was fish you were dining on then you had most of the cat population to accompany your repast. It took a very hard heart to ignore these half-starved beasts, even though you tried not to because it caused a hazard for the waiters trying to negotiate between tables with overladen trays in their hands and a menagerie of cats underfoot. But in the end, those sad pleading eyes get the better of your concerns for health & safety issues and you relent. But the moment the food hits the floor the inborn survival instincts of these cute fluffy felines' kicks in and all hell breaks loose as the cat equivalent of a squaddies free-for-all ensues. Those that were once silent now screech and hiss and claw at each other for the smallest of scraps, with the kittens normally coming off worse as they were always going to be the last in the pecking order. But man loves the underdog or undercat in this instance, and the older ones would be shooed away while the best bits of lamb or chicken or fish would be hand fed to these sweet little things that would one day themselves grow up to be top of the cat pile and would no longer be deemed cute enough to warrant being fed so lovingly.

    I began to wonder where all these felines emanated from every lunch and dinner time as they were nowhere to be seen for the rest of the day. It was then, while nonchalantly gazing around the taverna in between courses, that I noticed the ceiling moving? This was, in fact, a sort of rush matting affair that was strung underneath the proper vinyl roof but which created a space in which the local cat population inhabited. At first, it was quite fascinating to watch this suspended ceiling expand and contract in places as if it were breathing, not realising it was caused by the movement of the cats as they walked gingerly across it. Once explained by Thomas the reason for this strange phenomenon the fascination increased as you wondered how strong this matting was? I had visions of some poor unsuspecting patron suddenly became a maniacal cat juggler as a whole litter of kitties dropped on them from a great height!

Dinner was always completed with a complimentary Kumquat offered at the end of the meal. This we also fell in love with! Sweet and glowing amber in the candlelight, it was a perfect end to a perfect feast. Thomas's became our nocturnal retreat for most of the holiday and we made sure we reserved the same table every evening for the following night's gastronomic foray.

With our hunger sated we traversed the beach admiring the handful of small one and two floored villas that nestled the shore. These were a mixture of old and new builds of differing colours.

A couple were private dwellings belonging to locals but the rest were rentable properties owned by various holiday companies.

"If we can ever afford it," I said to Julie, "We'll rent one of these. Imagine waking up by the sea and breakfasting on the beach?"

There was no argument from Julie.

We wended our way back up the many steep steps to our apartment where we sat out on the balcony, imbibed more wine, breathed in the pungent peppery aroma of the cypress trees and listened as the last sounds died away from the music that played in the bar far down below us. This was replaced with the soothing rhythmic ebb and flow of the sea and the cooling, gentle breeze blowing through the bay. No words were spoken lest we broke the spell.

The next day began with cappuccinos. We had already placed our towels on a spot just in front of our now customary haunt, and retired to a shaded table to relax before………relaxing! Thomas, Alexandra and a few other Greek patrons were already deep in conversation when we arrived. One of them, Nicos, a tall, slim, perma-tanned 40 something, ran the gift shop behind the taverna which was also owned by Thomas. He spoke little English and spent most of his day behind the shop's counter watching a small black & white TV that seemed to play endless game shows. As we sat drinking in the day and the coffee's we listened as their discussions went from being an amiable chat to becoming very excited accompanied by wildly animated gesticulations, so much so that to us it seemed an argument had broken out, but it is just the Mediterranean way of expressing themselves. Back home, raised voices and flailing arms were normally a leaning to a full-fledged punch-up. Here, it was just emphasis.

Dimitrie, the morning waiter, served us with a warm smile and a 'Kalimera', that you knew he meant. Dimitrie was 20ish, tall, skinny and somewhat bucked toothed. He spoke fluent Greek, English, Italian and a smattering of Russian. It also turned out he was a professor of music! He was always cheerful and never tired of us or the countless other sunbathers enquiring if it was going to be another glorious day.

"It's Kalami," he would reply. "It's always beautiful, whatever the weather!"

You couldn't argue with that logic.

As we sat sipping our cups of milky froth sprinkled with cinnamon a giant four-masted yacht hove into view and glided silently and effortlessly through the iridescent water heading north to who knows where. The colossal white canvas sails billowed and ballooned in the early morning air stream that journeyed up the channel as they hauled the gleaming hull ever onwards. In stark contrast, a ferry en-route to Corfu town emerged from the left, throbbing and metallic. Its wake churned and frothed as it ploughed through the brine, taking no prisoners. This was not built for grace, just for purpose. We watched for what seemed an eternity as the illustrious craft cruised noiselessly past our bay until finally disappearing around the headland. The ferry already forgotten about.

There were few on the beach this early in the morning so our first couple of hours were spent privately and quietly. Until we were joined by Ben that is! We had seen him on the beach every day since we arrived, sometimes with the same people, other times with somebody different. He was never alone and nobody ever took offence to him, even when he was uninvited. He was very amiable with a charm about him that endeared him to all. Today, it was our turn. Before we even acknowledged his presence he had plonked himself down between the two of us without so much as an excuse me. He sat staring silently at us for some time before finally laying his head down and stretching out for a nap, the way dogs do. Ben belonged to Thomas's brother, Dimitrie, who owned a taverna back along the main road leading to Kassiopi. As it was too dangerous for the dog to be that close to the traffic Thomas would bring him down at the beginning of the season to the safety of the beach. Here Ben would spend his days wandering back and forth between Kalami, Kouloura and Agni beholding to no-one and friend to all. He knew he would always get looked after food and drink wise for nobody could ignore that sad imploring look that dogs do so convincingly. Those that did ignore him only did it the once for he never patronised their company again.

By now the sea was wide-awake with odd fishing boats, pleasure craft, pedalos and swimmers. Single masted yachts and twin-hulled catamarans drifted serenely into the bay to weigh anchor in preparation for a languid lunch. Amongst all this, skimming effortlessly across the surface of the ocean, sail puffed and board gleaming, came Pete. Once the captain of the skies, now the master of the seas – albeit on a smaller scale. He never flew them but to Pete, his surfboard was his Concord; his Memphis Belle; his Spitfire. When he rode the waves, he was airborne once more.

There was another new sound now, a deep, pulsating thrum. We scanned the horizon for the source of this strange noise but could see nothing. Thinking that perhaps it was something more vehicular we gazed up toward the road, but again, nothing! We were puzzled, confused, perplexed?

Suddenly, what can only be disguised as a fast-moving cylinder came into view from our right? We strained our eyes and shaded our vision from the sun to make out the sleek outline of a hydrofoil as it skimmed effortlessly across the water like a giant, mechanical water boatman. This high-speed vessel made the 55min crossing to the island of Paxos and, apart from the ferry from the mainland, was the only way to reach the island as there was no airport.

As we lay on the loungers we became aware the waves were becoming noisier and busier, but we ignored it and carried on with our blissful relaxation. Suddenly, what can only be described as a mini tidal wave, hit the beach. Fortunately, our loungers kept us above the waters but our belongings, including Julies phone and a digital camera both in her bag underneath her, became immersed in the brine. Panicking, we managed to retreat up the beach while rescuing our now sodden clothes and waterlogged possessions. We stood in bewilderment, along with Ian & Leslie & Jeanne and countless others who had been caught out, proffering different suggestions as to its cause.

"Oh, that happens every time a ship passes" offered Ian.

It seemed the logical explanation but I wasn't convinced. As quickly as it came, it receded, and Kalami returned to normality.

We spent the rest of the day with one eye open on the lookout for large vessels sailing past the bay. I logged every liner and ferry that passed and waited for the resultant tsunami to engulf us again, but it never occurred? This puzzled me and proved that Ian's prognosis was incorrect. So, what had caused the sudden swell? I came to the conclusion that the waters of Kalami were as laid back as Kalami itself and that occasionally it would notice the comings and goings of the world hurrying by. The ferries! The speedboats! The aeroplanes! It would look at all this, not caring for mans rushing ways and just shrug its shoulders in indifference; thus causing the surge.

After our mishap, we returned to our apartment to change our clothes and repair our electricals. Unfortunately, neither the phone nor the camera were responding to our efforts of drying so we left them indoors where the sun shone in and decided to partake of the high-level swimming pool at the other end of our floor rather than walk all the way down to the beach again. Here was also quiet, with the odd sunbather and water-bather patronising the elevated pool. We ordered a couple of drinks from the bar and stood at the railings overlooking the bay. Corfu town shimmered in a heat haze many miles away while ferries and liners of every size and description passed each other on their way too or from the port. Immense white-sailed yachts and tiny single engined fishing boats were doted here and there, hardly seeming to move. We felt as detached from the rest of Corfu as we did from Albania.

We watched as the swallows frolicked and gambolled as they searched for food for their young. Soaring and swerving, chasing and plunging, they would race through the blue skies, skimming over rooftops and darting between cypresses in their relentless search for insects. We spread our towels on a couple of white plastic loungers, stripped down to our swimwear and crashed out to the melodic background music emanating from the bar. Little by little we were coming to accept that perhaps we had indeed found our paradise.

After some time Julie went for a dip to cool off while I was too far relaxed to want to move. The mid-afternoon sun was now beating down relentlessly and I sought the shade of the parasol. My cold beer now warm, I fought with the urge to either join Julie in the pool, refill my glass or just lay here enjoying nirvana a little longer. Eventually, the heat beat me into submission and I decided that being cooled off externally was probably more effective than internally, and so I joined her in the pool. I should have known that by now she would probably be speaking to all and sundry and sure enough there she was, immersed in deep conversation with an older couple at one end of the pool. She introduced me to Pam and Don who, incidentally, lived only an hour or so away from us in Jaywick. My reluctance to get too involved reared its ugly head again, but the more I chatted to Don the more interesting I found him. He was a retired plumber of the old school, adept in all aspects of the trade but also an expert in the use of all things leaded. Plumbers of today are only proficient in copper, steel and plastic pipework. But Don was also skilled in the art of moulding and sculpting sheet lead into any shape or form desired. An art lost on today's modern plumbing fraternity. I knew from that point on that Don and I, indeed all four of us were to stay firm friends.

Being in the building game myself, I could ally with Don. We spoke for ages on all things constructional and mechanical. What we had most in common is that in most things we were self-taught. Working on building sites gives you a great opportunity to watch and study different tradesmen ply their art. Sometimes this was done surreptitiously, other times blatantly. On occasions, you would get the chance to ask questions. Quite often you would get a civil answer, other times abuse. In these instances, you would just watch from a safe distance. The only art I could never master was plastering. Regardless of how many times I watched, how many questions I asked, how many times I attempted to emulate, my efforts were abysmal. I eventually conceded defeat and now leave it to the experts.

Morning broke as it had done every day so far, hot, bright and offering nothing and everything, depending on your mood. We opted for nothing. No day trips. No sightseeing. No visiting. No shopping. No hassle. Today we would make amends for yesterday's frivolous activities. We bedded down in our usual spot, in front and just to the right of Thomas's, and there we stayed until done to a turn. Having learnt our lesson from the first couple of days on the beach we made sure we were far enough back from the water's edge in case of sudden surges. We weren't disappointed. A little while after lunch we were aware the sea was becoming restless and gathered all our belongings off the pebbles and onto our loungers. Sure enough, some 10 seconds later the beach was partially engulfed by another mini tsunami, soaking all and sundry who were unaware that occasionally the sea just sighed a deep breath, shrugged its shoulders and then settled back to being part of this Nirvana.

By 4 o'clock we had returned to our apartment, deposited our beach gear, changed and headed out along the Kalami road to Agni, the next bay along. We had been told there was a footpath that ran along the cliffs edge and up and over the promontory. This we duly found after turning off the road just as it ends as a private drive. We followed this down a steep, rough concrete track leading down to a dilapidated single roomed house, surrounded by an overgrown vegetable garden. We skirted this and found ourselves on a small beached cove. Evidence of human habitation was piled up in the form of empty beer bottles, cans, plastic bags, fag packets and other assorted debris. I never ceased to be amazed that, even in the surroundings of a near paradise, mankind blights a natural beauty with his own flotsam and jetsam like an animal marking its territory!

We joined the path a little way along the beach as it climbed up to follow a narrow trail edging along the outcrop. Precarious in places we finally found ourselves descending into Agni bay. Here, along a short stretch of beach, were the four tavernas serviced by the sea taxis that picked up their patrons from the small jetty in Kalami. It was a bay very much like Kalami but on a much smaller scale. It was pebbly with a few loungers for hire but if you ate at a taverna you could use their loungers for free. As it was late in the afternoon when we left, and now into early evening, we decided to have a quick drink and head back. By this time we reasoned that it was too dangerous to attempt the rocky path back again as the light was fading, so instead we opted for following the road out of Agni to pick up the main road back to Kalami. A piece of cake!

An hour later we had only managed to get as far as the main road as the route out of the bay was extremely long and steep, but once met we found ourselves with another dilemma. From our vantage point, we could see to our left a main road far below that disappeared into the hills but going in the right direction, likewise the traffic on it. But the road we were now on also went in the right direction but didn't look to be a major road. Do we follow this road and maybe end up in the middle of nowhere? Or do we walk all the way down to the other and then perhaps find out we were on the right road in the first place? We um'd and er'd, debated and procrastinated, paced back and forth for what seemed an age.

"What the hell do we do Dave?" Julie asked, knowing the answer.

"I don't know Juls, don't ask me!"

"I thought you said you'd seen this road on the map before we left?"

The onus was now firmly on my shoulders because; a) I had mentioned the road, and b) because I'm a bloke! We had three options. We could return to Agni and hope they would allow us to travel back on one of the sea taxis that were only for those that dined there? We could turn right but that may lead us to God knows where? Likewise, if we turned left! Suddenly, just as we about start flipping a coin, a car appeared coming up the hill from the direction of the lower road and we recognised it as one we had seen some time ago below us. As it sailed past we breathed a sigh of relief that we were on the right road, for it turned out that this and the one below were one and the same road.

Relieved, we set off on what proved to be a dangerous undertaking as the road was very narrow in places, with rock face on one side and sheer drops on the other and with no footpath anywhere! At times we had to hug the rocks as coaches and lorries passed with only inches to spare. As time and distance went on with no sight or signs for Kalami we became worried again that perhaps we had made a big mistake and that this wasn't the right road after all? As we neared a small group of houses on a sharp bend I noticed one with lights on, door wide open and a TV blaring that looked like a small shop. I knew no Greek but I'm sure if I just kept repeating Kalami and pointing that I would be understood. I was expecting to be met with either indifference or open arms. What I wasn't expecting was their Ninja dog! He lay in the shadows unseen and blending, awaiting passing idiots such as myself to stray into his territory, his domain. I neared. He sprang! I was surprised that, even though I was physically drained at this point, how quickly I could cover 50yards in less than 3 seconds. Fortunately, Ninja dog had forgotten the leash firmly tied to his collar that halted his attack abruptly and just stopped me from running in front of a passing lorry. Curious to his sudden outburst, the shopkeeper emerged shouting something which definitely wasn't Japanese but which the devil dog understood anyway. Giving me one last contemptible look it slinked back into the shadows from which it had emerged. The shopkeeper looked at me without speaking and I began my attempt at Greek charades.

"Kalami?" Point, point, point. "Kalami, yes???" Point, point, point.

He gave me one of those 'bloody tourist' looks, nodded and disappeared inside.

"Are we going the right way?" Julie asked.

"I think so? I bloody hope so!" I replied.

As we tramped on we were aware of how clear the night sky was. This was mainly due to there being no ambient light from any street lamps along most of the road as there were none. This made our travels even more dangerous as the only thing liable to be picked out by ensuing headlights was a couple of bits of pink flesh. Eventually, we came to a piece of road we recognised from our first day and the drive from Corfu town. A stretch of road, bordered either side by houses and shops, narrowed down to a single lane and traffic had to be controlled by traffic lights. This lifted our hearts and our spirits for we now knew for certain that we were heading in the right direction! Our pace quickened and our backs straightened at the thought of our destination coming ever closer. A few hundred yards out of the town and darkness fell again. We rounded a bend with olive trees high up to our left overhanging the side of the road. Suddenly, a guarding bark emanated from somewhere in the trees. I froze. Having already encountered one fiendish dog, were we just about to be attacked by some rabid wild beast this close to home? We had two choices. We either cross the road and hope we don't fall over the barrier to our doom? Or I send Julie on ahead first!! In the end, we stood still until the barking ceased and then very gingerly and quietly, tip-toed along the road. Every few yards saw us coming to a sudden halt as the barking would start up again, each time getting closer and closer. As there were no fences atop the high walls surrounding the olives I had visions of the dog suddenly leaping vampire-like off the top to sink its teeth into my neck!

Once past and out of danger we accelerated to a near run. Some ten minutes later saw us passing Dimitrie's Taverna that sat overlooking Kalami. We knew then we were on the home run.

When we finally opened the door to the apartment it had gone 11 pm and we had missed dinner! It had taken us three hours to walk back from Agni, a journey that had taken us just 30minutes along the cliff track going and less than five minutes by boat! In that time I had been attacked by one dog, threatened by another, squashed up against rocks by a coach, nearly flattened under the wheels of a lorry and been ignored by every passing motorist since our journey began. We sat exhausted on our balcony, downing glass after glass of wine to steady our nerves and handfuls of peanuts to sate our hunger.

As we sat recuperating an ironic, if not strangled version of the Beatles hit 'The Long and Winding Road' was emanating from the karaoke night in the bar far below us. We both had a slight chuckle to ourselves before fatigue finally overcame us and we collapsed into bed. We drifted off to the soothing strains of the waves lapping the shore and a strange but comforting single noted call sounded by a creature of the night. We fell asleep holding hands and heard no more until morning.

Despite last night's arduous debacle, we rose just after dawn. We breakfasted on fresh fruit; coffee for Juls, lemon & ginger tea for me. We sat and watched a near glass sea broken by the occasional wake of a fishing boat returning with the morning's catch. Corfu port and waterfront could be seen quite clearly from our balcony, as could the forts old and new. Huge white liners berthed offshore awaiting their turn to dock. Not so the ferries, their continual comings and goings never ceased. The lure of Corfu town beckoned and we decided to book a seat on the sea taxi excursion that left late afternoon. It was due back again at around 8 pm so we booked our usual table with Thomas for nine. England was playing an important decider that evening so I was hoping to get back to watch at least some of it.

4 o'clock found us waiting at the small jetty along with eight others. Our transport arrived at the appointed hour and we boarded. It was a fast motor launch which the pilot insisted in demonstrating to the full. Once away from the bay he would open her up full throttle causing the bow to rise up out of the water. Then, which he found utterly amusing, he would suddenly shut the engines down causing the bow to drop. The effect was to be suddenly drenched with the resulting spray. Oh, how we laughed?

From sea level, we could see all the bays we had passed by bus from a different aspect. Nissaki beach with its large hotel nestled between the rocks. The villas huddled among the cypresses on Barbati beach. The long sandy coastline of Ypsos backed onto by the main dual carriageway and parades of shops and tavernas. The tree-lined and gardened promenade of Dassia. The bay of Gouvia with its yachting harbour. Each cove as different as the next.

We docked in Corfu harbour and disembarked, slightly damp but none the worse. We were told to be back sharp at 7.30 for the return trip. Miss it and it was an expensive taxi ride back! We now had three hours in which to explore the town. As with most we headed straight for its heart and were met with a maze of narrow side streets and alleyways. We opted for a side street which eventually brought us out we knew not where? Rather than turn round and retrace our path we instead trusted to luck in the hope of finding our way back. Before long we found ourselves in the middle of a labyrinth of back streets. We nipped up alleyways and turnings at every opportunity, but somehow always ended up back in a street that looked familiar, but then, they all did!. We were beginning to feel like we were in an episode of the 80's TV series The Prisoner, where no escape from 'the village' was possible! Eventually, we emerged on to a street busy with people and breathed a sigh of relief. We didn't know where they were going so we just allowed ourselves to be carried along through an endless maze of shop-lined streets and alleyways until we found ourselves deposited close to the portal we'd entered through a couple of hours earlier. Worried about getting lost a second time we found ourselves a café close to the harbour and decided to sit out the rest of our time with a bottomless pot of coffee and watch the town and ships pass by until 7.30.

Once back on board it was the thirty-minute ride back to Kalami, along with the customary splashing of the tourists which the pilot still found amusing but very few others did! Once reached, the male contingent quickly disembarked in search of a bar showing the England game. We found ourselves doing the same but only because we had already arranged to meet Ian & Lesley at the Dimitris & Fossos apartment's bar. When we arrived it was standing room only around the large screen TV. We quickly grabbed a drink and I squeezed in beside Ian to hopefully watch our national team reign victorious. It wasn't a very exciting game, lots of tooing and froing but not a lot of action! A few minutes later we were awarded a free kick, to be taken by the golden boy of the day, David Beckham.

"How long has it been since he last scored from a free kick?" I asked Ian.

Moments later it was in the back of the net.

"About three seconds!" came the wry retort.

They went on to win the game boringly but comfortably and national pride was once more restored.

Game over, the poolside bar emptied as quickly as it filled as reserved tables at the three tavernas were occupied, swelling the half-empty eating places to near capacity.

After a late dinner, we returned via the Cocktails & Dreams bar where karaoke night was in full swing. We decided to have one drink and see how long we could endure the agony of well-loved songs being put through a grinder. A couple of would-be Britney's and Beyonce's did their best to out-screech the local cat population before a 30 something guy, dressed head to toe in black, took to the mike. We had seen this 'dude' around a few times looking like an extra from a spaghetti western, complete with black leather cowboy hat, ponytail and goatee, black shirt and jeans finished with black leather boots. All this in the fierce Corfu sun! We waited for his rendition of Rawhide or to start whistling the theme from The Good, The Bad and The Ugly. Instead, he amazed us all with a near-perfect performance of Frank Sinatra's New York, New York! We sat in silence, as did about 60 other patrons. When finished, he was treated to a cacophony of whistles, cheers and rousing applause. He accepted this all with a dignified bow and returned to his friends at the bar looking rather nonplussed at the ovation. Unfortunately, he was followed by another cat strangler so we decided this was the perfect time to retire to our apartment.

As usual, we sat on our balcony, drinks in hand and stripped down to our undies in the balmy Corfu night air. It was midnight as the last wailing notes of Hi Ho Silver Lining from the bar entourage faded into the dark. We were safe in the knowledge that all was at peace now as this was the closing downtime for the bars. Then quietly, the melodic tones of the singing cowboy struck up once more. We sat listening intently as we were serenaded with his version of My Way. Whether he was goaded into performing one last time, or maybe he just wanted to leave the crowd on a high after some of the embarrassing recitals, we'll never know. Regardless, he definitely brought a perfect end to the evening this time, not only courting appreciation from the patrons in the bar but he also received a few cheers and applauds from others sitting on their balconies also.

"Hi Julie, Hi Dave!" Pam greeted us as we lay prostrate in our normal spot.

"Hi, darling!" was Julie's reply. "What you up to?"

"Well I thought I'd come down to the beach for a change But I'm not sure what Don's got planned?"

"Pull up a lounger and sit with us" offered Juls.

"No, it's ok, I don't want to intrude."

"Don't be silly!" I replied. "We would welcome the company!"

Pam duly sat and before long the two were immersed in lengthy girly conversation. I was starting to get itchy feet and, as Don hadn't emerged, decided to leave the girls to their gossip and Grecian sun and go exploring. I'm still an old backpacker at heart so wandering off and investigating is in my blood.

I had been told that if I followed the road out of Kalami it passed by a small harbour called Kouloura where another single taverna could be found. Follow the coastline round further and another bay, Kerasia, could be located. Again, with just one taverna but with the auspicious (or inauspicious?) connection with the Rothschild's estate which was situated just a few yards up from the beach. Curiosity got the better of me. I bade goodbye to the girls and headed off, tracing the road as it leaves Kalami. As it climbed, broken panoramic views were glimpsed between cypress and elm. Both below and above me, villas of varying styles and colours dotted the landscape, all vying for the best views. Bougainvillaeas, resplendent in their creams and crimsons, peach's and gold's, violets and maroons, were draped over any spare wall that could be found. Chrysanthemums and crocus's lined the road and cyclamen grew like weeds.

After about 10 minutes the road bent sharply left to climb the hill to the main road. Branching off this bend the road drops down for a couple of hundred yards then hairpins back to fall steeply down to Kouloura harbour. I bared left at the hairpin and descended along a track to the stony beach of the bay. Here, in this off the beaten track cove, there was still the customary loungers and parasols, but no takers. The track became single person narrow as it rose sharply from the beach and followed the coastline. Passing first through cypresses with its heady peppery aroma, the undergrowth soon became gorse like and dense in places. The path undulated, sometimes precarious, other times dangerous. As it levelled off, heather and bracken abounded. Here and there shapes could be seen moving in the undergrowth. Some large, some long and thin, but all were elusive and hidden. I reached a point where a sign, pointing upwards at a near 45°, read TO THE MAIN ROAD. Not only was the pathway totally indiscernible but a machete and crampons would be required to attempt any ascent!

About an hour after leaving Kalami I finally reached Kerasia, descending steeply from the path onto the beachhead. This was a fairly long bay with the taverna situated at the other end. The beach itself was relatively flat and wide, backed onto by a few rentable villas. There was one small shack type shop selling the usual tourist paraphernalia and cotton wear. I sauntered lazily along the shore, passing bathers of both sun and sea, and lunched at the taverna. The only road rose steeply out of the bay passing the expansive estate of Nathaniel Rothschild to the right, nicknamed Chateau

Rothschild by the locals. Here the privacy of many visiting dignitaries, oligarchs, royalty, moguls and our own government and shadow government ministers, including the leaders of both main parties, was protected by high walls and unseen sentinels. Their seclusion and secrecy were further maintained by a private jetty allowing the only real and safe access to the domain. It became apparent that most of the huge, luxury yachts and launches that we drooled over as they passed Kalami were destined for this retreat. They say that money talks. Here, it screamed.

I sunbathed for a while on some rocks by the taverna watching ferries and yachts pass by unaware of my existence, then headed back. Before long I came across the direction sign again and noticed a small, seldom trod path that led down to a small rocky inlet. Once down, flip-flops and T-shirt were removed and I sat with feet dangling in the warm, crystal clear waters. Here was peace. Here was solitude. Here was Nirvana.

I had no towel with me nor swimming trunks, but I cared not. I emptied out the pockets of my shorts, wrapped everything up in my T-shirt and placed them to one side. I then spent a very pleasant solitary half hour floating in my very own sensory deprivation tank, devoid of any ambient influences. As the Ionian washed over me, cares and qualms were carried away with the ebb and flow of the tide. I wasn't in Corfu, I wasn't even in this life, I was existing betwixt worlds. I was aware of everything and nothing. I *became* everything and nothing. I was completely detached from my body, floating not in the water, but in a different dimension. Was this what an out of body experience felt like? If so, I had no intention of returning. What sounds and smells there were became enhanced but my shell of a body was numb. I could feel no waters around me. Was I floating? Was I flying? Was I still here? I didn't want to find out. I was happy where I was. Lost in my own bliss.

It was only the deep, prolonged hum that disturbed me. A strange, low vibration, rather than a note, that emanated far off. It ceased as quickly as it started but then repeated itself a little while later. It was more distinct this time. More purposeful. It penetrated deep into my soul and stirred my thoughts, causing them to become more rational. The third time shook me from my meditations and brought me back to this reality with a start. As I regained my bearings and senses I glimpsed the huge liner slowly passing the bay, sounding its horn to warn or acknowledge another liner approaching from the north. I cursed this intrusion; I cursed the liner; I cursed the Captain. But no one heard me.

Now firmly ensconced back in this reality, I swam back to the rocks, removed my shorts, squeezing as much water from them before donning them again. I retrieved the rest of my belongings and climbed back up the small path to rejoin the high-level trail. I needed no towel for the sun would dry me in no time at all. Before long I was back at Kouloura and then Kalami. Julie and Pam hadn't moved an inch from where I left them.

"Still here?" I enquired.

"Yeah, haven't moved all day, have we Pam?" Pam just opened one eye and nodded.

"Did you meet Don on your travels?" Asked Julie

"No! Was I supposed to?" I asked, surprised.

"He took a walk round to Kerasia as well!" Said Pam, now propping herself up on one arm, looking slightly worried.

"Well, I never passed him." I offered. "How long ago did he leave?"

"About an hour ago!" They replied together.

"He went round to buy a pair of cotton trousers from the shop there. You don't think something's happened to him do you?" Pam asked, now sitting up.

"About an hour ago? Ah, that was probably when I went for a dip on the way back. He wouldn't have seen me from the track, it's too high up. He's probably been to Kerasia, bought his trousers and is on his way back by now." I offered, consolingly.

"Hope so?" Said Pam, now worriedly looking out to sea.

Every few minutes one of us could be found scanning the road as it rounded the bend in the hope of a glimpse of a familiar face. The more we looked, and the less we saw of him, the more anxious we all became. No words were spoken, but the air was full of unease. I knew there had been reports of people falling from the high cliffs to their deaths on a couple of stretches of the walk, but I obviously kept this to myself. 'Should I go and look for him?' I thought, but this would probably alarm Pam even more so. No, best just to act as if nothing's wrong. If she saw I wasn't worried then this might placate her. My mind started racing. 'How do you ring for the Coast Guard out here?' 'What's the number for the emergency services and do they speak English?' 'Would they just laugh at me and tell me not to bother them until tomorrow?' Being the man I was probably expected to take charge of the situation, organise search parties, synchronise the entire islands emergency services, give trauma counselling to those affected, contact the British consulate, all the time still wearing my underpants on the outside of my costume!

45minutes later Don could be seen walking down the road through the trees. Pam visibly relaxed, as did we all. Before long he arrived smiling and proudly showing off the slacks he'd purchased, not realising the concern and the near international incident that he'd caused through no fault of his own.

That night the four of us met up to experience the authentic Greek entertainment show at the Cocktails & Dreams bar. It proved to be a highly engaging night of traditional and modern folk dancing replete with much high kicking, knee bending, arm linking and an abundance of exuberant "Whopa's!" This is an expression used extensively in all Greek dancing and is always guaranteed an even louder "WHOPA!" buy alcohol-induced audiences.

Also, traditionally, there was the fire dance. Lines of flammable liquid from squeezy bottles are sprayed onto the ground and ignited while members of the troupe dance in and around the flames. Many a time a dancers shoe would be bathed in blue flame as they stepped in the burning liquid, but this was soon extinguished through fast and fancy footwork. The crescendo to the evening's entertainment was to get as many of the audience as possible involved in a conga type line, weaving in and out between the tables and themselves with a plethora of "WHOPA'S" being offered, in and out of time! It was a joyous and entertaining evening where Greek, English, German, Swedish, Russian and a smattering of other nationalities came together, as much for the music and dancing as for the alcohol. Here no boundaries existed for there were good and bad 'artistes' from every race. Through dance and song, a common language was formed.

The day started as it had done every day, full of sunshine, azure skies and cobalt seas. From our balcony could be seen a lone swimmer traversing the bay. Below us, the gardeners were watering the flower beds and the cleaners were sweeping the pathways. Swallows, already awake long before man, were busy serving a breakfast of insects and grubs to their young as we consumed our fruit cocktails and sipped tea. Very little stirred in Kalami save for a delivery lorry and a lone car heading out of the village. It was a work day for Corfu and in the distance sawing and hammering could be heard on an unseen building as smoke rose lazily from a fire hidden amongst the trees. We felt another lethargic day looming.

When we could finally tear ourselves away from the serenity of the morning we headed down to the beach via Thomas's for our cappuccino fix before dumping our now tanned bodies at the water's edge. Today was going to be a nothing day. Nothing was planned; nothing was contemplated; nothing was happening. Today we were gonna do nothing!

Shortly were joined by Ian & Lesley, followed some 10minutes later by Jeanne & Peter, replete with windsurfer. As this was their last day, they had plans of nothingness also. We lay like six gingerbread men browning in an oven. Occasionally one of us would stir and plunge into the shallows to cool off before collapsing back onto our loungers as if it was all too much effort, which it was. Even the sea today was lackadaisical, so apathetic that it couldn't even be bothered to shrug! It really couldn't care less today. It was that sort of nothingness.

"Have you tried Dimitri's yet?" enquired Ian
"No, haven't had the chance yet" I replied.

"That's OK then cos we booked you a table for tonight. We were in there last night and reserved you a lovely table on the balcony overlooking the bay. We booked for 8. Is that ok? "

"Fine," we both said, slightly surprised.

"Well, I know you'd spoken about it so we thought we'd sort it for you as it's quite popular and we know Dimitri very well."

"Thanks, Ian, we look forward to it!"

By lunchtime, Pam and Don had sauntered down to the beach and joined us for a light snack at the taverna. This was also their last day and, as we didn't think we'd see them again, we exchanged numbers and addresses and promised to keep in touch. We did this the following year when we were visiting Clacton for the day. Unannounced, we turned up on their doorstep, stayed for the afternoon and have remained firm friends ever since.

Lunchtime rolled into afternoon, afternoon into early evening. We said our goodbyes and, as Julie walked back with Pam & Don, I went with Peter & Jeanne to their private apartment where they gave me a few bits they didn't want to leave behind plus a handful of fresh lemons that they picked that morning from the tree in their garden. We exchanged addresses, shook hands, promised to stay in touch and wished each other bon voyage. I returned to our apartment where I found Julie tearful that good friends were leaving.

"I'm sure we'll make others," I said, consoling her.

"I know," she said, "but we all became so close."

"Come on, let's get dressed for dinner." I tried to sound upbeat. "I'll treat us to a fancy dinner at Dimitri's. Order anything you like, it's on me!"

By 7.30 we were out of the apartment and treading the main road some 500yds along to Dimitri's restaurant. We didn't have to walk as he actually lays on transport to come and pick you up but as it was such a short distance we felt stupid to order a lift. As it was, being picked up would have been the safer option as, even at this time of night, the road was still busy and no pathway existed. Still, we made it in one piece and, true to Ian's word, were shown to one of the best tables in the establishment.

The ambience of Dimitri's was matched only by the position and views it affords, perched high at the top of the Kalami valley with sweeping, unobstructed views across the tops of the sentinel-like cypresses as they marched en masse down to the sea. The views across the promontory to Corfu town were even more impressive, so too the expanse of Ionian as it swept southwards.

It was a night for spoiling ourselves. I feasted on Shitaki mushrooms with a béchamel sauce, a rare sirloin steak and a rich chocolate gateau, all washed down with a sophisticated burgundy. Julie also opted for the mushroom starter but followed with sea bass and a fruit cocktail dessert, arguing that it constituted one of her healthy five a day portions. She was more conservative with her wine, choosing just a couple of glasses of chardonnay to accompany her repast. Had I been a smoker then now was the perfect time to light a large Cuban Havana, sit back with a brandy and drink in the vista. But unfortunately I wasn't, nor did I like brandy, so I opted for a port instead but still drank in the ambience.

"Are you sure we can afford this?" Julie asked, a little worried.

"Don't worry," I replied, dismissing her doubts. "It's my treat so I'm gonna stick it on my credit card and worry about it when I get home."

By now the daylight had faded and in the valley, a thousand lights accompanied our candle. On the far shore of Albania, orange lamps illuminated roads that climbed up into the hills and disappeared. And here and there, among the blackness of the nocturnal sea, a handful of red and green dots pinpointed lone fishing boats plying their trade. The night was still and close, the air perfumed by tree and flower. Below us, the vale dropped steeply away into inky blackness. Above us, a myriad stars pinpricked an unceasing black canvass. Somewhere, amongst the olives, a Scops owl called, breaking the silence of the moment.

After much debating, we made the agonising decision to vacate the taverna and carry on our appreciation and imbibing back at the apartment. I called for the bill and proffered my credit card for payment. It was a lot more than I bargained for but we were on holiday so no expense spared. I loaded my card into the machine and the waiter entered the amount owing. He returned it to me for verification (and tip) which I duly added to the bill. I punched in the PIN number and returned the machine so he could see what a generous tipper I was. I drank some more port and smiled at Julie as I waited for the card and receipt to be handed over. She returned a contented smile.

"Sorry sir, your card has been declined."

My smile vanished.

"Pardon!" Obviously a mistake I thought. "It should be ok, that's the correct PIN number and there's enough to cover it?"

"It's saying refer to bank."

"What does that mean?" I asked, nervously.

"I don't know sir. I'll try again for you."

I was starting to get a little panicky now. I knew the card had sufficient limit so it must be a fluke.

"Sorry sir, it's been declined again. Do you have another card?"

"I don't understand, I've used it recently back home and it was OK. I don't have another card!"

Julies smile had disappeared. I was now beyond panicking and into speechless territory. What the hell was I going to do? I had no cash on me and no other cards. I had visions of being beaten up by irate Greek waiters and thrown over the side into the abyss! Or being arrested and left rotting in a Greek prison for the next 5 years!!!

Salvation came in the form of a now unamused wife.

"Here," she said begrudgingly, "use mine!"

This the waiter did and it went through without any problems. I breathed an embarrassed sigh of relief and thanked her profusely.

"I seriously don't know what's wrong with it Juls, it was fine back home. Do you think someones hacked into my account and emptied it?"

"I don't know Dave, we'll have to find out when we get back," she said, rather peed off at having to pay for such an exorbitant meal out of her own money.

When we did return I phoned the bank to be told that, as I hadn't informed them I might be using my credit card abroad, they stopped it in case it was a fraudulent transaction. I was both relieved and annoyed at the same time.

Unfortunately, the escapade with the card put somewhat of a damper on what had been an otherwise enchanting evening.

Chapter 4

Lazy Lunches

The morning found us and a handful of others waiting on the main road for the tour coach to take us on the one and only excursion that we had decided to book on the holiday. My sister, who regularly stayed in Sidari, had recommended that, if we get the chance, we should visit beautiful Paleokastritsa on the north-western coast. She'd extolled its countless virtues and backed them up with a myriad of photos. Beautiful it certainly looked.

With countless stops along the way, it was a good 1½ hours before we reached our destination. When we did finally arrive surprisingly the coach didn't stop by the beach, where we expected it to, instead it followed a very steep and narrow winding road up to the Theotokos Monastery, perched high on a rocky promontory overlooking the bay. For such a small church the car park was surprisingly large and filled with numerous coaches of differing nationalities. I wondered if there was a scam going on between the monks and the drivers. They make sure that all sightseers are automatically taken to the monastery, regardless if they want to or not, and in return, they are guaranteed a good spot in heaven when the time comes?

It wasn't an imposing monastery by any standards but its elevated location proved to be its salvation. Although the current buildings date from the eighteenth century, it is believed to have been established as early as the thirteenth and is still home to seven monks. In amongst the small church were a mixture of icons of Christ and George and the dragon which puzzled me for I couldn't understand why our patron saint was being depicted in a Greek monastery? But then I'm not a theologian nor a historian, so what do I know! Also among the small estate was a tourist shop selling a plethora of religious paraphernalia and olive oil, a wishing well that now accepts Euros, and beautiful paved gardens resplendent with bougainvillaea, vines, marigolds and geraniums. You didn't have to be religious to appreciate the splendour or the meditative qualities of this mini garden of Eden. It had an inherent spirituality about it that rose above anything sacrosanct.

The tour over and the driver blessed, we were driven back down the steep road, passing hoards of equally puzzled tourists being driven up. We finally disembarked in a purpose made coach park and were confronted by countless little stalls lining the main street and squeezed into every last inch of space left along the monastery road as it tapered down to a single lane before the climb. Every tourist whim was catered for here from lacework to olive wood jewellery; T-shirts to towels; 'authentic' Armani and D&G leatherwear to flip-flops; baklava to soap. Looking forward was a breathtaking vista of rocky outcrops, blue sea and golden sands. Look behind and it could have been Southend.

Somewhat famished we perused the countless cafés and tavernas before stumbling on a small pastry shop offering cheese and bacon pies, pasties, and all things to be found in an English bakery. Not surprisingly it was run by a lady from Birmingham who, separated from her husband, had decided to join her sister in Corfu and then to set up a mini bakery. Her success was measured by the almost bare shelves and hot cabinets, and it wasn't even lunchtime yet! We purchased one of the said bacon and cheese pies to share but which was so tasty we went back and bought another! With this and a diet coke, we strolled down to the beach area, hired a couple of loungers and basked in the midday sun watching brave/foolish teenagers climbing the rocky outcrops and then 'tombstoning' into the bay. There were a couple of boats offering trips around the bay and into caves and grottos under the cliffs. The photos on their display boards looked impressive and inviting, so I boarded one such boat leaving Julie sunbathing as it wasn't her thing. When the craft was full we set sail, all with cameras at the ready. Some 30 minutes later we were back having visited not one single cave! We were shown plenty, but visit them? No! Disappointed I rejoined Julie on the beach where we just had enough time for a coffee before the coach departed to carry on its tour of the area.

A short time later we departed the town and began to ascend the steep road up to a point called Bella Vista. About halfway up we passed through a small village that clung to the roadside, leaving the coach only a couple of inches either side between its wing-mirrors and the walls of the buildings. In this situation, cars coming down through the village would give way to anything coming up, except in this case a stubborn/stupid middle-aged woman in a Fiat. She met the bus head on and refused to budge. Irate gesticulations and harsh Greek words issued from the coach driver and pedestrians alike, but she wasn't going to budge. Eventually, the driver had to get on his mobile and await someone to come down from Bella Vista and persuade this woman that it was impossible for the coach to back up and that she had to give way. By this time she was out of her car and, with arms flailing and head nodding furiously towards the coach, she was giving all and sundry a piece of her Greek mind. Finally, after much shouting, finger pointing and reasoning she eventually saw the light and backed up, letting not only us through but three other coaches a dozen cars and a donkey as well, all giving her the evil eye as they passed, including the ass!.

    Once reached, the views from Bella Vista were stunning. At the top was a glass-sided café/restaurant bearing the same name with an extensive veranda offering an unspoilt 180°panorama. This was a goldmine for the owners. Daytime offered unhindered views stretching far along the rugged western coastline and out as far as the horizon. In the evening, astounding sunsets could be witnessed as the fiery red star sunk into the blue Ionian. It was difficult to leave such beauty but leave we did as we were due to visit a kumquat distillery on our journey home, much to the annoyance of at least half the sightseers as England were playing a World Cup qualifying match that evening and most of the male passengers were expecting – hoping – praying to be back in time. Very few of us were that interested in the distillery as all we were really shown was the kumquat grove and the finished product with a very brief history of how the fruit was brought to Corfu from China. We weren't shown how the fruit was crushed, fermented, distilled or bottled, only what it looks like when it's ready to buy! Which seem to be all they were interested in and was probably another scam involving the coach drivers or, more than likely, they were related, as most Corfiots seem to be?

By the time we returned to Kalami it had gone 8 o'clock, England were 1-0 down and we were starving. Luckily enough we found a table at Thomas's, dined heartily, drank deeply and eventually slept contentedly.

"Kalimera David!" "Kalimera Julie!" The greeting was genuine and warm and always with a smile.

"Kalimera Thomas. Another beautiful morning!"

"Of course," Thomas laughed, "It's Kalami! Two cappuccinos?"

"No. Cappuccino for me but could we have an iced lemon tea for Julie please?"

"But of course. No problem."

And it wasn't. Nothing is ever a problem here.

Thomas hadn't always owned the taverna. Kalami was originally a fishing village and Thomas was born and raised here a fisherman, like his father Spiros. He never contemplated leaving the village; the love for his family and its people was too strong an attraction to take him anywhere else. As he grew older an opportunity came his way that allowed the entrepreneur in him to surface. In 1985 Pepe's Taverna, owned by his Grandmother's brother, became available. Thomas, along with Alexandra, could now combine his two loves, that of fishing and Greek cuisine, making piscine dishes his speciality. Thomas's Taverna was now born. Since then he's been blessed with a loyal clientele who return year after year.

We had decided that the next two days were gonna be spent doing absolutely nothing but sunbathing, swimming and chilling. We walked nowhere, visited nothing, spoke hardly to anyone. Except for the evening that is.

As a change to Thomas's, we decided to give the taverna round at Kouloura a go. Apparently, it was also noted for its extensive variety of piscine dishes as freshly caught fish in abundance is delivered daily. We got there early and were seated at a table under a pergola that overlooks the small harbour. From here, more northerly views of Albania were on offer, as was the stretch of coastline that I had traversed on my way round to Kerasia. Apart from the taverna, there was a gated property and two small whitewashed, blue-shuttered cottages with front doors that opened out onto the narrow road that ended where the harbour wall began. If you have made the unfortunate mistake of driving down this road, then the only way back up the hill is to reverse all the way.

Kouloura from the coastal path

The evening was a mixture of relaxed voices and cheery waiters interspersed with the put-put-put of small one-man fishing boats as they came and went. From our viewpoint, we could observe them trailing their nets beneath the harbour entrance in a large semi-circular movement. Here and there small rafts sat anchored as their owners, rod in hand, patiently watched and waited for the tell-tale sign of a disappearing float. Here, they fished in the same way as they had done for countless generations before them.

We began our feast as normal with wine, the first mouthful always being the most pleasurable. We shared mixed starters of hummus and tzatziki, a mixture of yoghurt, cucumber and garlic, which we lavished on our thick sliced bread. Bread always accompanied every meal, whether asked for or not. By the time the starters were finished, we already had a feeling verging on fullness, and the main course was yet to come! When this was brought to our table we both wondered whether we had over ordered. As if my main course of stifado, huge chunks of beef in a rich red wine sauce with pasta, wasn't filling enough, it was also accompanied by chips! Julie's dish of red snapper was rather more conservatively served with rice, but our side order of courgette fritters definitely caused consternation between us. Could we – should we finish it all? We tucked in and tried our best. By the end of the repast, a handful of chips and half of the fritters remained untouched. We both sat back and straightened our bodies in the way that you do, thinking, hoping, it will create more room in your stomach if you stretch it out, but it never does.

By now, all that could be seen of the fishing boats were the small white running light atop their masts, bobbing and swaying on an unseen ocean. Bill paid and wine finished walking back up to the road was our next challenge. There was no shortcut or taxi service, just a long walk up a steep hill. The trek back to Kalami took twice as long as the outward journey. Admittedly it was dark now with most of the road unlit and, apart from the road out of Kouloura, most of it was flat or downhill, but we were stuffed and the capacity of the meal weighed heavy on our footsteps. Fortunately, we didn't have to negotiate all the steps back up to our apartment as there was a lift for the less able and the over-indulgent. Unfortunately, it only took you as far as the third floor so we still had a bit of a climb left to do.

We fell in through the door, exchanged evening wear for something more comfortable, by that I mean anything that expanded, and collapsed on the balcony chairs like two beached whales. We lasted another hour before the heaviness of the meal and the headiness of the wine led us willingly into the arms of Morpheus.

We were woken by sun and song drifting through the open patio doors. The sun needed no explaining. The song was courtesy of one of the

Greek cleaners as she greeted the morning. The words I couldn't understand but the emotion told all. I couldn't see her but I knew she was smiling as she sung. The intonation, the rhythm, the pitch said more than the words ever could. I didn't need to know Greek to know this was a song of joy, of love, of beauty. The feeling was infectious.

This day saw us venture up the coast to Kassiopi, a picturesque one-time fishing village on the north-eastern corner of the island, now renowned more for its harbour frequented by luxury yachts and hire boats. It has accustomed itself with grace to the tourist industry and is a rare example of somewhere that tries to be all things to all people, and succeeds. Its history can be traced back to Roman times, being patronised by Cicero, Mark Antony and Emperor Nero himself. Remains of a once Roman/Venetian fort overlooks the town where fishermen's abodes have now been replaced with apartments, tavernas, bars and assorted tourist shops. Countless other harbours of this ilk succumb to the tackiness of the tourist industry, but Kassiopi has managed to retain its charm and individuality.

Life still centres around the harbour, as it has done for hundreds of years. Every May 8th a ceremony takes place to commemorate the miracle of a young 16th-century boy, blinded for stealing and then regaining his sight by staying in the local church overnight. All the locals congregate on this day at the same church where they are given half a loaf of bread, they then proceed down to the harbour where, amid dancing, music, wine and much celebration, whole lambs and pigs on spit roasts are carved and the breads are filled to capacity. By the end of the days feasting and drinking I should imagine most people resemble the young boy, except their blindness, would have been alcohol induced!

The beach is situated a few hundred yards along a narrow road that circles the coastline and which emerges at the other end of the town. Steep steps lead down to a smallish pebbled shore festooned with loungers and parasols. As with Kalami, the water is crystal clear and warm and encompassed by two rocky peninsulas. We spent a good couple of hours there doing the usual before venturing back into the harbour for lunch. Choices for eating were plentiful and varied and we opted for a small taverna right on the harbours edge. So close in fact that you could look down and watch the fish swim endlessly around in the hope of the odd scrap of food finding its way into the water, which invariably it did. But this was more to amuse the diners seeing 20 or so fish fighting over one crumb of bread rather than any interest in the marine life.

Lunch took an age for we were in no hurry. Boats came and went. Yachts passed by. Fishermen offloaded their catch. Locals sat watching and musing. All under the sleepy gaze of the harbour. There was no need of haste here, try as hard as you might, you could not rush Kassiopi.

Kassiopi

It was with great effort that we eventually relinquished our table to explore further the streets and alleys of the town. Apart from the road down to the harbour, there were only two other streets of any importance to the average tourist. This was the road leading into the town, and the one leading out. And, as they were both one-way streets, basically there was only one road! Food-wise, a variety of tastes were catered for; Italian, Chinese, Mexican, British, as well as traditional

Greek food could be found along the main streets and around the harbour. These, along with the cafés and bars, brought the town alive in the evening time. One taverna we noticed was offering two starters and main meals for the price of one in the evenings, so the following day we decided to forego the delights of Thomas's for a change and caught the late afternoon bus back to Kassiopi. Being too early to eat we strolled the already walked streets and revisited the same shops frequented the day before. Cinnamon sprinkled cappuccinos were sipped from a rooftop café bar overlooking the harbour while we chilled and fantasized about owning one of the floating luxury apartments that masqueraded as a motor yacht, all the time just whiling away the hours until dinnertime. We had noticed that one of the restaurants along the harbour front was named the 3 Brothers' Taverna. The owner of the bar informed us that many years ago, three desperate brothers wanting to escape from Albania, swam some three miles across the Ionian Sea to Corfu where they settled in Kassiopi and opened a taverna. They were eventually joined by their mother and father and the taverna's been there ever since.

    When we could daydream no more we sidled down to the allotted taverna to dine. We did so to the diverse strains of music emanating from the many varied bars and eateries that, although contrastingly different, somehow strangely complemented each other. As the taverna was central to the harbour we had an unrestricted near 150° view of the coastline of Albania, with its far mountains and grey mottled hills sweeping down to the sea. As liners and ferries crossed back and forth along the distant shores, ablaze with lights from bow to aft, the evening fishing boats departed Kassiopi to their night's hunting grounds. We feasted lazily for there was no need for hurrying, even if you wanted to. Our hunger satisfied we strolled around the harbour once more to soak in the last of the evening's tranquillity before heading back up to the main drag to grab a taxi as the last bus departed at 5.30. Fortunately, there was one at the rank and we hired it for the journey back to Kalami. It was a warm pleasant evening with the sun already set behind Mount Pantokrator, so with windows open we reclined in the back of the Mercedes as it drove unhurriedly along the twisting road to our destination when the driver suddenly pronounced

"You're lucky people!"

"Why?" we enquired puzzled.

"Because there's only two taxis in Kassiopi and the other one had gone to Corfu Town. Had there been an airport run then none of us would have been here. You would have been stuck in Kassiopi overnight!"

Once again it was brought home to us just how much we assume things to be just like home. There, the buses run till late in the evening because demand dictates, and if you can't get one then taxis are two a penny. In Corfu, the demand is for those wanting to get to and from work and tourists just happen to be extra revenue along the way.

When we arrived at our destination there was another evening of Karaoke taking place in the bar. We didn't need to visit to experience the vocal attributes of the 'entertainers' as every note, every cadence, every word drifted up in the still night air. Some we giggled at, some we grimaced, some we disbelieved! But then the unmistakable tones of the man we dubbed the singing cowboy wafted sweetly around a hushed audience. This time a Dean Martin number was covered and covered extremely well. He was awarded the usual rapturous applause when finished and we sat awaiting the next poor wannabe who had to try and follow him. Understandably it was some time before anybody summed up enough courage or supped enough alcohol took to the mike. Even though I mocked them I secretly admired them for they had the guts to do something I would never do, no matter how inebriated I was.

As usual, the music ceased at midnight and the next half hour was full of the sounds of happy revellers wending their way back to their apartments or villas. We sat for the next two hours listening to the natural sounds of the surrounding fauna accompanied by the gentle lapping of the waves on the beach. Occasionally a lone worker from one of the tavernas could be seen driving out of the village on their way home, their beams like two searchlights in the inky darkness of the unlit road. With Kalami at peace and the world at rest, we slunk away to our beds, too scared to make a noise in case we woke up Corfu.

We only had two days left of holiday now and decided that we had done enough visiting, walking, boating & excursioning and that, until we left on Tuesday, we were just gonna chill and get back to what we did best – sunbathing, swimming, sunbathing, lunching, sunbathing, reading, sunbathing etc. By the time Tuesday came around we were bronzed to perfection and gleaning admiring glances from those that had just turned up looking like we did two weeks ago.

Our last night in Thomas's saw our meal pleasantly interrupted by a travelling quartet of musicians. A portly gentleman played the accordion while two others accompanied him on acoustic guitars. The fourth, and youngest of the troupe had the most important job. Even though his contribution musically was just to keep time with his tambourine, come the end of the medley of well known Greek tunes and songs, it was his job to visit each table with his instrument collecting tips from the happy tourists. As he did so the other three would follow him, quietly playing their instruments, beaming huge grins and bestowing many an 'Efharisto' as money was dropped willingly into the tambourine. Once done, they regrouped at the back entrance, finished their last number and departed to an appreciative round of applause. Moments later they could be heard entertaining the patrons at the taverna White House.

     Meal over we said our goodbyes to Thomas and Alexandra and said we'd see them again in 12 weeks time. At this Thomas's said to me that when we come back he'll take me out on his fishing boat! I nodded, thanked him then panicked for the next 12 weeks as I was no fisherman, in fact, I had no interest in fishing at all!! I kept thinking of ways to get out of the embarrassment I would suffer when he realised that I was a complete numpty when it came to anything angling wise! I kept my fingers crossed that he would forget.

Julie had been down all morning at the thought of leaving this idyll and by now she was in tears.

"What's the matter, sweetie?"

"I don't want to go home!" she conveyed between tears.

"Me neither, but unfortunately we have no choice?" I said, comforting her.

Such was the effect Kalami had had on us. In those two short weeks, we felt that we had gone from being tourists to indigenous.

"I know," she replied through sodden eyes, "but I still don't want to go. Don't worry; I'll get over it."

The drive back to the airport was full of happy memories but tainted with unhappy thoughts. Julie was thoroughly miserable, as was I, at the thought of having to leave this Eden; this Arcadia; this Utopia. Every turn and bend exposed another tree-lined, topaz blue bay, dotted with Corfiot/Romanesque style villas, making our leaving all the more difficult.

Then a thought occurred to me.

"Don't get too downhearted sweetie, we'll be back in 12 weeks time!" I said, more upbeat.

"But that's a lifetime away!" Julie replied.

"It will soon pass though; look how quickly the weeks flew past waiting for this one."

It worked. She rested her head on my shoulder and was lost deep in thought of our return.

Corfu airport is pretty basic. Queues for the ticket desks stretched from one end of the airport to the other. If you were unlucky, you had to queue outside along the pavement. Once through to the departure lounge there was only the duty-free area, a café and a couple of shops to peruse. Seating was at a premium and the information screens refused to give information. There was also no air conditioning which explained the strange seating area outside the terminal consisting of a number of plastic seats under a canvas roof. We thought this was an overspill area but realised too late that this was actually the coolest place to be. Too late! We were trapped in the oven of a departure lounge now and there was no way back! The only respite came when a plane was to be boarded and the doors to the ramp were open to allow passengers to embus. For that brief time, half the departure lounge would sidle nonchalantly towards the opening for a quick gasp of cool, fresh air before being shooed away by security. The clever ones would join the queue of boarders, then make out they got confused when they got to the head of the queue but made sure their explanation was so involved that they could grab an extra few seconds of precious oxygen before being turfed out.

After much pacing and many toilet runs for Julie, our turn eventually came to be whisked away from our Shangri-la. We trudged down begrudgingly to the bus, drove 50yds to the plane and then dragged ourselves up the steps. A little while later we taxied to the end of the runway, paused momentarily and then accelerated sharply as we hurtled down the concourse before climbing steeply and banking left to follow the coastline north. In our minds, we silently ticked off the coves and bays in succession until we spotted Kalami. We held our gaze as long as we could until we could see it no more. Our hearts sank to be leaving, but we knew we had found what we were looking for.

We had found our paradise.

Chapter 5

Step back in Time

"Hairete Thomas!"

Thomas looked up from his paper, taking a moment to remember us.

"Hairete! Hairete! Good afternoon David & Julie. You are back!!"

"We told you we would be Thomas!"

Warm handshakes and kisses ensued.

"It seems like you just have only gone!"

And it did. Twelve weeks had passed since our last sojourn, but it felt like we had never been away. It was eerie. It was as if the past three months never existed. Like we'd gone up to our room and just overslept a little. Nothing had changed, but then we didn't expect it to. We just carried on where we left off back in June.

"Cappuccino and lemon iced tea?"

"You know us too well Thomas!"

We pulled a couple of chairs out from a table towards the front but just far enough back to be under the shade of the vine-covered roof and settled back into Kalami. Nothing about the vista had altered, except for the differing boats that visited. To our left, two gleaming white catamarans; centre, a twin-masted yacht; and to the right an expensive, sleek sports cruiser. In stark comparison, the small, gaily coloured fishing boat owned by Greek George was tied in its usual mooring at the end of the old concrete and wooden jetty. The old lady who hired out the loungers and parasols was sat quietly under a makeshift sun canopy, ever watchful for punters. Nobody escaped her. No matter how far away from her you were, she would spot you and be on you for payment before you had time to lie down! She also carried with her a club hammer and spikes for those wishing to hire the parasols for she knew that, try as hard as you might, it was impossible to drive an ordinary umbrella into the pebbly beach and have it stay upright. I know; I tried! In front of her sat the handful of pedalos and canoes, rented out of course, by her. The blue lifeguard tower, as usual, was empty and Ben the dog, unusually, was laying on his own by the edge of the walkway.

  As if on cue, a sudden surge of water rose up the beach to greet unsuspecting sunbathers, as it had done us some 14 weeks prior. We both chuckled to ourselves for it as if it was done for our benefit as if to say it knew of our return, but it wasn't bothered.

Dinner that evening was something special. We dined at our usual table at our usual taverna but it had been a full moon the night before and tonight was still in complete luminosity. The black mirrored surface of the water reflected its iridescent brilliance like a silver ribbon floating in the darkness. At each wash of the tide, the light encroached onto the beach a little more as if trying to reach us before being pulled back again to play among the waves. The evening air was humid and still. Somewhere among the trees, a single Scops owl called lending a magical essence to the night. There was no need for candles on the tables, the moon-glow permeated into every shadow. Had a mermaid appeared swimming in the radiance none would have been surprised.

The meal lasted a lifetime for we wanted to savour every last moment of the evening. All three courses were relished slowly. Half carafes became full carafes. Every wave was scrutinised as it washed onto the beach. Watched intently as it began its journey inland, gathering momentum and volume as it rolled along the shore until reaching a crescendo of silvery white surf before expelling itself and receding back into the depths from which it came, never to reappear as the same wave again. Had we been smokers we probably would have got through a full packet between us as an excuse to draw the evening out even further. Eventually, we succumbed to the heat of the day, the heaviness of the meal and the headiness of the wine and, begrudgingly, called for our bill. Thomas returned with our change.

"Will you join us for a drink?" I asked.

"Yes, thank you," he replied, "but please, have these on Thomas."

We didn't argue.

As we sat talking he told us of one of his business plans.

"I have a magazine about Corfu. All about its people, its culture, its food, its customs. Everything!" he said. "It is called it My Kerkyra because this is the Greek word for Corfu."

He then proceeded to show us the glossy publication full of pictures and articles, none of which we understood as it was all in Greek! He could see the puzzled look on our faces.

"I want to do one in English," he said. "Do you think people would read it?" He asked with an excited look.

"Very much so," we both replied. "Sounds a great idea! When is it being launched and how do we get a copy?"

"Very soon," he replied. "Maybe the end of the year."

He gave us a subscription form which we duly filled in. By Christmas, we had received our first copy of My Kerkyra which we now subscribe to every year.

Our efforts of lengthening the evening exhausted, we reluctantly traipsed back to the apartment to savour as much of the evening as possible from our balcony before tiredness finally dragged us to our beds.

We were greeted with rain as we woke.

"This can't be!" said Julie. "This is Corfu. It's not supposed to rain here!"

"Even paradise needs a little watering from time to time," I replied. "And you can't have a rainbow with the rain!"

It wasn't heavy but enough to put paid to any sunbathing ideas we had. Instead, we opted for catching the early bus to Kassiopi and then on to Sidari. We ascended the steep steps up to the main road and queued by the side of the road opposite the bus stop. This is an odd little Corfu, if not Grecian, quirk. Instead of having bus stops on both sides of the road, they have them on just one side and you stand opposite them on the other side for the bus going in your direction! This obviously cuts down on costs re materials, labour and time of having to construct two, but it means that in extremes of weather only one set of passengers gets the benefit of a shelter, as in our case this morning. After a few minutes, we were joined by others who had forsaken the beach for an excursion instead. When the bus did finally arrive it was greeted by a dozen or so drowned rats who were not a cheery bunch. Dripping and miserable we boarded for the ten-minute drive to Kassiopi. Once there we were deposited at the square to await the bus from Sidari. There was no shelter here either and it was too risky to chance going for a nearby coffee just in case we missed it.

Fifteen minutes later we were wet but Sidari headed. We only went because my sister, a regular visitor to the town, was forever extolling the virtues of its charm. We probably wouldn't have bothered had the weather been better.

Our first warning of what was in store came from the site that greeted us as we stepped off the bus. There, in all its garish plastic unsightliness was a McDonalds! It had all the cold charm of those back home including the same problem with litter. Everywhere you looked there was a discarded McDonalds item, be it packaging or food. We looked at each other, then the bus timetable and then at our watches. Damn! We had an hour to wait before we could return! Fortunately, the rain was now just a drizzle so we girded our loins, mustered our resolve and set off to explore the rest of the town.

The majority of it bordered the main street. There were the usual shops selling the usual tourist tat, plus a tattooist and beauty salon. But here restaurants and bars proliferated. There was no real pavement to speak of so you shared the road with the traffic. Every bar was open and all, bar none, offered a full English breakfast for a handful of Euros. As we passed each bar these breakfasts were being devoured with relish by heavily tattooed, large gutted, England T-shirt wearing patrons dripping with chunky gold chains and signet rings. The men were worse! Had you replaced all the Sidari signs overnight with Benidorm, no one would have noticed! Sounds bitchy I know, but the epitome of how other nations envisage the English abroad is encapsulated here.

    The sun was now shining down on Sidari as if to brighten the place up. It didn't. We cut through a side street to a wide sandy beach in the hope of escaping the litter cluttered streets. What we found was a litter cluttered shore instead. Not happy with just treating the town with disdain, the same Neanderthal mentality was exhibited here also. Empty beer cans, discarded cigarette packets, broken glass, fast food containers and used condoms were found in abundance. To walk barefooted was to court grievous injury. We walked the length of the beach but nothing changed. Cutting through one of the bars and back onto the high street we headed back to the bus stop knowing that shortly we would be escaping this blight. When we left Sidari it had started raining again but much heavier this time, as if even God wanted to clean the place up. I overheard somebody on the bus refer to Sidari as 'looking like Blackpool, but on a bad day'. I think that's an insult to Blackpool! To be fair, when I later spoke to my sister she did say that we'd missed the best part which was the Canal D'Amour, just outside the town, a series of sandstone promontories that created small sandy inlets, nothing like Sidari at all.

Unfortunately, we didn't get that far so we'll never know.

Around 10 mins later the clouds broke and the sun shone bright and hot again. We didn't want it to be a totally wasted day so we opted for stopping off at Roda on the way back. We were dropped off near the beach, a long sandy affair, considerably nicer than Sidari. We lunched and strolled. As we perused the few shops fronting the beach a small van approached slowly, its tailgate up and a loudspeaker system issued forth the voice of a man who sounded like he was asking for help in committing suicide. It was a low, flat but commanding voice spoken in one tone with no inflexion or cadence whatsoever. Was this a political party election broadcast we thought? It sounded drab enough! Or some kind of warning telling people to keep off the streets because of a toxic cloud heading our way? It sounded dire enough! We didn't speak Greek, how would we know? As he passed the truth was weirder than our guesses. He was selling carpets! His whole van was stacked up with rolls of carpets and rugs hanging out of the back door. Not one person took notice or even seemed slightly interested as he drove slowly past. But then again, if that was his sales pitch he was more likely to attract people wanting to dispose of a dead body!

We wandered up to the main street to check out the bus stops and found more shops lining the road. We walked and window shopped before coming across a small shopping mall that had a sign up pointing the way to the Little Tea Pot tea rooms. Intrigued, we wandered in, climbed some steps and walked straight into the 1940's! The chairs were spindleback dark oak with drop leaf tables delicately covered with lace tablecloths. In one corner a small raised stage housed a Chesterfield drop arm settee, a gramophone player, a barley-twist standard lamp, a walnut writing bureau and a bow fronted display cabinet. The walls were adorned with pictures and photos of singers and movie stars of the era while Glenn Miller played softly in the background. We ordered cakes and teas and these were duly delivered on a wooden trolley, with bone china tea service and a three-tiered cake stand. The lady who ran the tea room heralded from Lancashire and had come out to Corfu after getting divorced. She bought the premises, opened the tea rooms and has never looked back. She said it was even popular with the locals!

We left this little piece of nostalgia replenished and sated and went to find the bus stop for our homeward journey.

"Why don't we walk back to Kassiopi?" suggested Julie

"You can walk if you want to; I'm waiting for the bus!" I replied.

"It's not far........ is it?" she enquired.

"Far enough in this heat!"

Some 20 mins later the bus arrived and we set off. 9 ½ miles later we arrived in Kassiopi.

"Bit further than I thought!" admitted Julie.

"You don't say!" I replied sarcastically.

We strolled lazily around the harbour for a couple of hours and caught the penultimate bus back to Kalami. We felt justified now in being able to criticize somewhere we had actually been to, had seen with our own eyes and had experienced firsthand. It was somewhere we definitely wouldn't be going back to again.

The drawback of going this time of year is that it's mozzie season. Every night, both at Thomas's and in our apartment, anti-mosquito defences were used to the full but failed miserably. We sprayed our room with repellent; desisted from wearing any aftershave or perfume; installed an electric plug-in deterrent; lit citronella candles; ate plenty of garlic at dinner and burned incense coils. All these devices and sprays were guaranteed to work, but nobody told the mozzies that! They bypassed the incense, held their breath near the plug-ins and danced in the light of the candles before settling down for their nightly feast of human stuffed with Greek cuisine. Unfortunately, because of Julie's insistence on sleeping with the balcony doors open, I had to spend the entire night wrapped in the bed sheet with just my nose protruding to allow me to breathe. Sleeping was practically impossible for, just as I would begin to drop off, would come the familiar high pitched buzz sounding like a demented Kamikaze pilot on helium as a bloodthirsty mozzie would dive bomb me looking for a way in. But sometime during the night, my sheet must have slipped for I awoke in the morning resembling something from a Tom & Jerry cartoon. In all, I had amassed 25 bites to my head and face! I swore that that night that Julie would be sleeping out on the balcony!

To save embarrassment, I donned my sunglasses and a hat to walk down to the beach in the hope of covering as much of my face as possible. It didn't work. I could see the look on people's faces as I passed. I felt like I should have been wearing a bell round my neck and a sign saying 'UNCLEAN'!

"Is he alright?" people would ask Julie as though this terrible affliction had somehow struck me dumb as well.

"Mozzies!" would come back the reply.

This seemed to placate them and I would then gain sympathy – but no solutions.

The rest of the day was spent as normal but with quite a few more dips in the sea as the salt water was supposed to help lessen the bites. It didn't. Even Ben, our canine companion, who'd been visiting us regularly since our arrival, was ominously missing today. Was I that frightening!

The day had been quite changeable weather wise and by the time we settled into our usual table at Thomas's the sky was looking decidedly gloomy and cloud-laden. By the time we got our drinks, it had started spitting. Had the sky not looked so ominous we probably would have sat it out. Instead, we opted for moving back a couple of tables. This proved fortuitous for within five minutes the heavens opened and a deluge fell on Kalami. The little wooden tables that sat just out front of the taverna were forsaken as the downpour increased in intensity. Those that couldn't move to another table dragged theirs further in. The waiters leapt into action immediately and began furiously to roll down the heavy, clear plastic walls installed in case of such an event. Before long we were cocooned dry and warm in the taverna while outside a storm raged all around us. As we sat listening to the tumult raging against the roof and the walls, a sudden blaze of lightning streaked across the black sky lighting up the sea and Albania like a giant flashbulb. This was quickly followed by an ear-shattering clap of thunder, indicating that we were probably close to the epicentre of the storm. I had never experienced this before and I found myself mesmerized as I eagerly awaited the next explosion of light to illuminate the sea and the distant hills. I didn't have long to wait. Seconds later another flash, this time further round to the left, lit up Albania's shoreline and mountains and a couple of lone fishing boats in the darkness. As the rain teemed down the transparent walls potential diners could be seen hurrying along the beach obviously caught out by the speed the storm took hold. Within seconds they were outside the taverna trying desperately to find a way in. As the lightning flashed all around their profiles became silhouettes against the translucent walls. All and sundry rushed to their aid, pulling apart the plastic sheeting where it joined and beckoning them into a now full eatery.

The atmosphere became more convivial as the sudden claps of thunder brought forth shrieks from the women and children, and some of the men! This was followed by nervous laughter and much imbibing of alcohol for nerve-steadying purposes. Before long we were joined in conversation with a group on the next table, soon to introduce themselves as Jeff, his wife Christine, their adult daughter Adele and Christine's sister Jan who all hailed from Manchester. This was their first visit and they too had fallen in love with the place. They were all fairly well travelled and recounted many stories of exotic, far-off places, and also of other Greek islands. But they felt Corfu to be the best of them.

As the storm and the evening wore on and the wine flowed steadily, there didn't seem any point in trying to brave the elements, it made more sense to just stay put and enjoy the company.

Jeff in himself was quite an interesting person. It turned out that he was one of the first tutors for the Open University, although his looks belied this. He was a man after my own heart as he also liked camping and walking but, sadly, a heart bypass operation had now put paid to his annual pilgrimage with his daughter to the top of Scafell Pike in the Lake District every New Years day. Now suitably imbibed I ended up recalling, mile by mile, my conquest of the Pennine Way back in 1990. Between us, we bored the girls senseless.

It was around midnight before the storm abated enough to allow us all to vacate Thomas's and head back to our respective abodes. Ours a one-room apartment, theirs a spacious villa

We sat for at least another hour on our balcony watching the distant storm as it flashed and thundered far over Albania and mainland Greece. By now the precipitation had ceased and all that remained was the wonderful aroma that occurs when rain hits the ground after a hot, sunny day. Mixed with this were the saltiness of the sea and the heady aroma of jasmine, giving rise to a fragrance no joss stick or aromatherapy oil could ever match.

We awoke early to a greying sky and decided to venture into Corfu town again, but this time by bus. The previous night's storm, apart from being highly entertaining, had another bonus. No mosquitoes! The damp air had obviously curtailed their nocturnal sorties and I had slept a deep, unbroken sleep, free of buzzes and bites.

The buses from Kalami were infrequent and didn't really abide by any proper timetable. If it said the bus was due at 8 am then it meant anytime between 7.45 and 9. We opted for the 10 am which, surprisingly, was only 15minutes late. The journey was long and tedious and with many stops but eventually, we arrived around 11.30. We immediately checked on the last return bus and were told that it left promptly at 4.30. It was hard to believe that on a major tourist island of Corfu that is visited by hundreds of thousands of Brits every year, let alone other nationalities, that their national bus service comes to a grinding halt at

4.30. After that time it's either hire cars, taxis or if you're lucky enough to be on the route, a sea taxi. Regardless of tourists, Corfu moved at its own pace.

Having established return journeys we ventured into the winding narrow back streets of the town as before, except this time it was at a more leisurely pace where we could drink in the ambience and peruse at our convenience. We were met by a plethora of shops selling olive wood artefacts, Kumquat, cotton linen, lace and expensive jewellery, as well as the usual tourist tat. We were also met by a confusion of early Venetian, Roman, French and Neoclassical British structures, none smaller than three floors high. Some streets were so narrow that the occupants could probably exchange items from one window to another. And, curiously, nearly all the windows were festooned with shutters and all painted a dark green? Was this some local council prerequisite for living in these homes?

The loftiness of the buildings and the narrowness of the streets offered very little light in some quarters, which did nothing to enhance the drabness of the paint faded walls. Occasionally you would round a corner and found it opened into a courtyard. Here would always be found a small taverna or bakery with a few tables and chairs out front. Carefulness became a byword as, as narrow as they were, you would still find the odd motorbike or even car trying to negotiate its way through, brushing the stalls and pedestrians alike on its way through the town.

Greek Orthodox churches abounded. Whether squeezed into the narrowest of spaces or dominating a square, none were ever empty or closed, and there always seemed to be a service of one type or another being held. But this is a deeply devout Catholic race, born out by the numerous religious references to places on the island e.g., Aghios Stefanos, Aghios Ilias, Aghios Ioannis, Aghios Georgios, Aghios Mattheos etc. (Aghios/Agios meaning saint or holy). Also by the many roadside 'shrines' found all over the island. These ranged in design from simple glass and metal affairs to ornate mini churches normally about 12" square by 18" high that allowed a candle to be placed inside. Initially, I thought these were for those that couldn't get to church to worship or if they felt like a quick prayer on their way to work. I was put right by Julie, who was more widely travelled than me, as being dedicated to those who had died in road accidents. Their equivalent to the bunches of roadside flowers that now spring up all over Britain.

After the sometimes claustrophobic narrow streets of the interior, we suddenly emerged into a large, open paved area full of cafés and bars. This was the Liston Promenade. Once the boulevard to the nobility, now the avenue for the chic and moneyed. By day it is a quiet place to drink coffee, contemplate life or people watch. In the evening, it comes alive with music and night-clubs. Here could also be found the largest evidence of British occupation. A full sized cricket pitch! It was no Lords or Oval by any stretch of the imagination – there wasn't even any seating or stands, just a large grass area with a well-marked wicket. Begun in 1823 by the British garrison and Royal Navy, some 100 games are still played each year. The Corfiots themselves took to the game in 1825 and now boast many teams that meet regularly.

To the front, the Museum of Asian Art housed in a neoclassical building that was one the residence of the British High commissioners. Behind is the Esplanadae, Europe's largest square with a beach at one end and a bandstand at the other.

We stopped for a coffee and to watch the fashionistas parading their haute couture like the new aristocracy. Our worlds weren't too far apart. They with their D&G slacks; me with my M&S shorts. At the end of the day, you can't take it with you.

The Listons

As we again ventured deeper into the interior of the town the streets became wider and busier with proper pavements. The shops became more designer labelled, and the traffic became more congested. Likewise the pedestrians. We weaved and turned, twisted and backtracked as we made our way to the central park where all the local buses congregated. Here we found a tourist information centre and acquired a map of the town for ease of passage. Unfortunately, most of the street names on the map were anglicised while the street signs themselves weren't. This made life very interesting for now we could get lost in modern and ancient Greek!

We eventually found ourselves at the steep-sided, gargantuan walls of the New Fortress, towering above the town like some portly headmaster scrutinizing pupils in detention. Built-in 1576 during the 400 odd years that the Venetians ruled Corfu, it was a very old looking New Fortress. This was not to be confused with the Old Fortress built in the 13th/14th centuries, also by the Venetians, but with a bit of British workmanship thrown in around the mid-1800's. So we have the New Fortress looking old and the Old Fortress looking new!

Chapel of the Old Fortress

We paid our entrance fee and wandered the cobbled and flagstoned streets that led inwards and upwards. We investigated rooms, vestibules, halls and various quarters. All much of a muchness. I also find dungeons and underground passages fascinating but these were unlit and extremely dark and I had visions of disappearing down a large hole or well, so I decided to forego the temptation. Instead, we made our way to the top of the fortress where we were afforded expansive views across the dappled roofs of the town and up the coastline to north-eastern Corfu, taking in Mouse Island and the distant shores of Albania and mainland Greece.

Many photographs later we departed the stronghold and sought out one of the many cafés that proliferated the main streets, side streets, back streets and off streets. You could never die of thirst in Corfu town, only caffeine overdose. As we sat and drank in the cappuccinos and the ambience we suddenly became aware that we had approximately 15 minutes to get back to the terminus before the last bus left! We hurriedly paid and enquired as to the quickest way back to the depot. Directions were plentiful and confusing; some suggesting this way would be quickest, others suggesting that way. We decided to head back the way that looked most familiar quickly realising that all streets looked the same. We bobbed and weaved, ducked and dove until we eventually emerged overlooking the harbour where we turned left and headed back the way we remembered. By this time we were running as a €1.50 bus fare was much preferred to a €40 taxi fare. We made the bus with a minute to spare only for Julie to announce that she needed the loo, badly! I tried to bite my tongue as I could see our limited hard-earned spending money disappearing into the pocket of a smirking taxi driver. She vanished into the terminus café while I pleaded with the bus driver not to depart yet. He kept pointing to his watch while gesturing about timekeeping. How I managed to keep a straight face while he intimated about running on time I'll never know!

  A few moments later Julie re-emerged, running for the bus while trying hurriedly to adjust her clothing and me frantically looking at the driver and pointing in her direction. We boarded, sat down and breathed a sigh of relief while everybody else breathed an irritable tut. We trundled out along the harbour road and joined the main dual carriageway that headed back north. Stops were again frequent but the fares became a mixture of tourists, locals and school kids. It wasn't long before we were filled to capacity but that didn't mean more couldn't get on. Being the last bus meant you never left anybody behind unless they weren't Greek! Somehow, even though this throng of bodies, the conductor still managed to squeeze his way through to collect fares. The bus was now filled with a cacophony of Greek, English, German and Russian trying to be heard above umpteen different songs, tunes and drumbeats emanating from various iPods, walkmans and mobile phones of the school kids.

By the time we arrived back at Kalami, the bus had emptied out to just a handful of passengers. We disembarked and stood for a few seconds while we drank in the quietude of the bay and watched swallows soaring and dipping and skimming across the top of the water. We vowed tomorrow would we wouldn't be moving from the beach.

We made sure that we did nothing except soak up the still hot September sun for our last two remaining days. The week had flown by and the return to our inescapable lives was only 48 hours away. Nothing untoward happened. We met no-one, went nowhere, spoke to nobody – did nothing. On the penultimate evening, we once again partook of the weekly Greek night at the Cocktails & Dreams bar after enjoying our usual repast at Thomas's. The following day was exactly the same, bar the Greek night. Our intention was to chill as much as we could, so that's exactly what we did.

The final day was a morning full of Julie's tears again as we made our way down to Thomas's for one last cappuccino.

"Thomas, why don't you have a Greek night?" I enquired.

"I used to," he said, looking forlorn. "But the other tavernas complained that it was too noisy, so I had to stop."

"How stupid!" we both said. "Probably just jealous?"

Thomas shrugged his shoulders and returned to his office.

We sat in full sun staring out across the bay, neither of us speaking, but each knowing the others thoughts. A lone early morning swimmer traversed the cove and George, in his brightly coloured blue, red and yellow fishing boat glided silently to moor at the jetty. Ben, who we'd not seen since arriving, padded along the wooden walkway and stopped briefly for some fuss, as if to say 'Sorry I missed you!'. The air was still and hot and the sea becalmed. Only a faint ripple of the passing bather disturbed the glass-like surface. We sat in our own silence, not wishing to disturb the other in case our leaving was a dream and that by speaking it would bring us back to reality.

As our sad thoughts about departing our paradise projected out across the bay, a quite discernible roll of water could be seen some way off shore. It gave the appearance of a wave caused by something just below the surface pushing the water along as it travelled. We both spotted it and knew instantly what it was. It never increased in size or speed but stayed constant in its momentum. As it neared we glanced at each other and chuckled inwardly. A few moments later it crashed onto the beach, nearly reaching up as far as the walkway, before receding back to where it had come from.

We got up from the table, hugged Thomas and Alexandra, said our goodbyes and walked to the door. As we did, I turned and faced the bay and shrugged my shoulders.

Chapter 6

Asses & Arses!

The past seven months had been an eternity. A so-so summer had become a damp miserable winter. Christmas, Easter and a plethora of birthdays had passed and now spring was awakening. For us, it had slumbered too long. Foresight had helped to hasten the onset of summer by booking our return to Corfu as soon as we got back from last year's holiday. Flights that had changed from a Tuesday to a Monday were now on Friday, and the times were earlier. The departure from Stansted was now 6.20am which for us meant getting there at 3 am so we could book our seats together. Sleeping the night before was a waste of time for we were like two kids at Christmas waiting to find out what our big surprise was going to be in the morning. Except this time we knew what was in store for us, which made the waiting even more agonising.

As before, the hot Mediterranean sun was greeted by our Anglo-Saxon smiles as we stepped off the plane. Once the aroma of aviation fuel had died away we breathed in the sweet clean air of Corfu knowing that within a couple of hours Kalami would play host to two bleached bodies once again in desperate search of a Grecian pallor.

It didn't take long for us to hit the beach and the taverna. Thomas greeted us like old friends, his smile as warm as the sun. Kalami greeted us with indifference, but we cared not for we were home again.

As usual, our first 48 hours were chill-out days. The hours, the minutes, the seconds, took an eternity to pass, but we cared not a jot. Had we the power to halt time itself then we would do so in Kalami. It was a strange phenomenon that the days would drag from one to another but the holiday itself seemed to be over just as it began.

On the third day of our basking, we found ourselves laid up next to an older but not old couple. He, looking very erudite with his cravat, Panama hat and reading glasses hung around his neck; her totally opposite with straw hat and smoking roll-ups. It didn't take long for Julie to strike up a conversation. A few pleasantries were exchanged then she introduced us. At this, he, who had stayed relatively silent, sat up, swung his legs over the side of his lounger and stated, "I'm Reginald and this is Nips!" It sounded like something out of the comedy programme A League of Gentlemen. We tried not to laugh and spent the rest of the holiday trying to work out what Nips was short for?

Reginald was very well spoken, not so much born with a silver spoon in his mouth, more silver plated. He was a much-travelled man, having been the chief editor of a national broadsheet. His deportment commanded attention – his worldly tales likewise. He regularly espoused about all things nautical, giving the impression that sailing the seven seas was not alien to him. Nips, by contrast, was timorous and demure and overshadowed by her husband's demeanour. They were both retired and lived in rented accommodation, through choice rather than circumstance. Their reason being that they had worked hard for their wealth so, rather than leave it to their kids, they sold their house, rented a cottage in the country, had a Jacuzzi installed in the garden, and are spending the rest on holidays!

"Bugger it!" he stated, "Why should we leave it all for the kids. We want to enjoy it while we still can!"

A sentiment we could associate with. They eventually retired to their villa for lunch and the next time we saw them was at dinner that evening.

We were sitting at our usual table, totally unaware they were sitting at the table behind. We ordered our meals and wine when all of a sudden a posh, unmistakable voice piped up.

"Bugger me! Fancy meeting you here!"

There was no mistaking Reginald's accent. We turned and greeted them and past a few pleasantries. We realised they were just coming to the end of their meal so, out of politeness, we turned back round to let them finish in peace. The next thing we knew they had left their table and deposited themselves at ours! This would not normally have been a problem but our table was only really big enough for two!

It was obvious that Reginald had imbibed a few glasses of wine over dinner for he was now talking non-stop about all and sundry and not really make any sense on any of it. Occasionally Nips would throw in the odd "That's right!" or "Yes dear!" in reply to her husband's prompting on certain issues. We found them both very genial guests and Reginald when talking coherently, was a mine of information, most of it gathered on his many global expeditions as an editor. We would be sorry to see them go when our meals turned up but we needn't have worried. Without batting an eyelid they both carried on talking and drinking while we tried in vain to eat and chat at the same time. The small table became a confused mess of carafes, bottles, glasses, dinner plates, side plates, bread basket, cutlery, condiments and a candle. Throw in Nips's tobacco tin and Reginald's hat and there wasn't an inch of tablecloth to be seen!

Our dinner was suddenly but pleasantly interrupted by the arrival of the travelling musicians first experienced on our inaugural holiday. As Reginald was well and truly oiled by now there was no stopping his enthusiastic appreciation of their musical efforts. As one song flowed into the next so his clapping, foot stomping and attempts at singing along to Greek words that he didn't know became more fervent. People became more entertained by his antics than by the quartet in the end. Nips just sat there looking more and more embarrassed. Eventually, the tambourine was passed around, money deposited and Efharisto's and Good Byes given. Reginald eventually calmed down and Nips stopped being less discomfited.

As the hour was now late they decided to call it a night, leaving us with what was left of the evening to digest our meals and relax a little. They both rose to depart and Reginald produced his wallet to settle his bill. As he was sorting through his Euros he was totally unaware that he was starting to lean at an alarming angle towards the table. Just in time, I caught him before he tumbled headlong into what now looked like half the entire restaurant's dishes and glasses. He steadied himself, took a deep breath, then nearly fell backwards off the edge of the raised taverna onto the beach. Once again I just managed to grab him before he disappeared in a heap on the beach.

"It's ok, I'm fine! I'm fine!" he said indignantly.

Nips took control of him and led him out of the taverna before havoc was wreaked, much to the amusement of the other patrons, except those whose tables he was passing. As he neared each one on his exit the diners would instinctively set down their cutlery in case they had to make a grab for him for fear of him plunging head-long into their feast. The danger past, we sat ourselves back down, ordered another couple of drinks and spent the rest of the evening giggling about what had happened.

"Blimey!" I said, "We do meet some characters out here!"

Our thoughts were our own as we lay basking in the morning sun. Each care and worry fell away with every breath, and with every breath, you sunk lower and lower into the arms of Kalami.

After some time we became aware of a presence behind us. Looking round, Nips was sat on a lounger some eight feet back.

"Why don't you pull up a lounger and come and sit next to us?" asked Julie.

"I didn't think you'd want much to do with us after last night's debacle!" replied Nips.

"Don't be silly!" we both replied. "Come and join us!"

Hesitantly she moved forward, placing her lounger next to ours.

"On your own this morning?"

"No, Reginald will be along in a minute."

"How's he feeling today?"

"Absolutely fine. But then he always is!"

Moments later he appeared, strolling down the beach without a care in the world. He stood for a moment, surveying the horizon in his Panama hat before pulling up a lounger, he bade us a good morning and stretched out for a tan. Nips gave us a look that said 'See what I mean?' We felt it might be too embarrassing to bring up last night's little fiasco, so we didn't bother.

We lay for some time without speaking for few words were ever needed. You naturally absorbed the sounds and the sights and the smells. They permeated into your body until you became part of it. You felt that if you stood still long enough you would take root.

"Isn't it funny how every now and again the water suddenly surges up the beach?" Nips stated without warning.

"That's because it doesn't care," I replied.

They both looked at me quizzically.

"What do you mean?" Nips enquired.

"Kalami has stood here in one form or another for hundreds of thousands of years. It's seen civilisations come and go. Witnessed countless wars and cultural revolutions. Watched man care for and decimate the land. Observed the progression from fishing boat to ocean liner. Stood as man went from foot to flight. But, amid all these changes, Kalami just goes on being itself. It watches the comings and goings of man and occasionally just shrugs its shoulders at it all. And when it does, you get the surge."

"Very poetically put!" Said Nips.

After a few minutes of silence Reginald, without any indication that he was taking any notice said;

"See that headland on our right?"

Startled back into reality we all glanced starboard wondering what was taking place.

"Yes?" I replied for all of us.

"Abramovich has just bought that for five million Euros! Wants to build a casino on there but doubt if he'll get permission," he said, matter-of-factly, and went back to tanning himself.

With this small piece of interesting but useless information logged we all went back to doing nothing except lying there in our own thoughts. Occasionally I would check my watch to see if we were nearing lunchtime, but time never seemed to move. It was hard to get out of routines, to eat when you felt hungry rather than at set times. But if anywhere could break us of that, it was here. As we lay silent and motionless, Reginald suddenly declared;

"I'm going out on my boat. Anyone care to join me?"

Julie and I looked at each other, both thinking 'Bloody hell, he's got his own yacht!'

We both declined, swiftly using lunch as an excuse. We had seen how unsteady he could be on land; we didn't want to risk it at sea also. Nips also passed up the invitation, choosing instead to join us at Thomas's.

"So be it!" stated Reginald. "I shall sail myself around the coast for a couple of hours." And off he went.

We were a little intrigued to see this fine ship that Reginald would be sailing, having told us of his love for all things nautical. The tales of his many sea ventures and the variety of ships and yachts he had captained in his time made me wonder whether we were a little too hasty in passing up the opportunity to cruise around the island in style. Lazing on the poop deck of a gleaming, single-masted yacht or twin-hulled catamaran, and then wining and dining while anchored offshore in the deep Ionian did seem very alluring. But we had made our choice and now was too late as Reginald had disappeared off to board his vessel.

We lunched light on Greek salad and diet Coke, allowing the conversation to consume the time. It was the most we had seen Nips relax, not being overshadowed by her husband. She spoke lovingly about their time together and their travels around the world. As she talked of his passion for sailing, a small white motorboat entered the bay. Usually, this would have gone unnoticed but this one was steering straight towards the beach rather than the jetty. As it chugged nearer to the shore we could make out a figure in white, wearing a Panama hat, and waving. Reginald! Where was the yacht, the motor-launch, the catamaran? He beached the vessel, strode up the sand, took a mouthful of Nips wine, informed us he was going off up the coast to Kassiopi and promptly left as quickly as he had arrived! We all sat and watched as the craft disappeared round to the left of the bay on its way north. Nips just rolled herself another cigarette.

We never saw them again after lunch had finished. We can only assume they had returned home. Suffice to say, our meal that evening passed uneventfully.

Later, as we returned to our apartment, a familiar voice could be heard emanating from the bar. Could it be? Those dulcet tones. The silenced crowd. The Sinatra classic. Yes! It was the singing cowboy! There was no mistaking his vocal attributes. We quickly joined the admiring throng that sat transfixed as he serenaded them with 'San Francisco'. Why wasn't this man on the stage? He still looked the same as he had done seven months ago. Black boots. Black jeans. Black shirt. Goatee beard and black cowboy hat. As usual, he left the stage to rapturous applause, still looking embarrassed at the response.

We stayed for one drink then retired properly to the apartment. As usual, due to popular demand, he returned sometime later for a finalé, this time a rousing 'Fly me to the Moon'. If old Frank had been looking down, even he would have been impressed.

Clip clop, clip-clop.

We were waiting for the early morning bus to Kassiopi.

Clip clop, clip-clop.

There were about half a dozen of us standing in the bright morning sun.

Clip clop, clip-clop.

Some of us were gazing out over the bay; the others eyed the road in anticipation of the arrival of the bus. A tattered Greek flag hung motionless above the council offices of the Municipality of Kassiopi perched on a hill across the road.

Clip clop, clip-clop!!

Where was that coming from? All of us were now aware of metalled shoed feet on tarmac. But from where? Then, lazily, a lone donkey sauntered up the Kalami road, its head bobbing from side to side as it walked, oblivious to our presence. We looked for its owner following behind, but there was none. As it met the main road it stopped, allowed a lorry to pass by then trotted out into the middle and made off in the direction of Kassiopi! We all stood open-mouthed. Should we go running after the beast and risk scaring it off? Should we go and tell someone? But who? Then, from the same road, a gaggle of elderly Greek men and women, short of breath and red of face, sweating profusely and probably swearing just as richly, staggered up the hill as fast as their aged bandy legs could carry them. The women, clad all in black, were crossing themselves frantically while wailing Hail Mary's like they were chasing Satan himself. Had a funeral cortege passed they could have been hired instantly as rent-a-mourner. The men, wearing flat caps, open shirts covering a vest and shabby trousers held up by string, were more interested in retrieving the donkey and left the religious beseechings to the women. With hearts in mouths, we watched as countless lorries, cars and coaches steered around the errant burro as it wended its merry way along the road caring not for the traffic that passed either side. None except us seemed concerned. Eventually, it disappeared around a bend in the distance and we all hoped that somebody would have the presence of mind to stop and waylay it. Lagging someway behind now was the wildly gesticulating, wheezing entourage as they too ran up the middle of the road in hot pursuit of the escapee, looking not unlike a something from a Keystones Cop movie. This must have been a regular occurrence as not one motorist bibbed their horn, waved their fist or even looked remotely surprised by the site as they also swerved to miss the gaggling pensioners.

Our bus turned up some five minutes later. We all boarded and sat glued to the front screen hoping and praying that we wouldn't come across a mangled donkey carcase by the side of the road or, worse still, that we wouldn't be passed by a lorry coming in the opposite direction with an ass's arse sticking out of its front grill! Likewise for the pursuing OAP's! Fortunately, no such spectacle greeted us and we can only assume that somebody did eventually intercept the animal and led it off to a field somewhere. Again, likewise the OAP'S!

A couple more halcyon days came and went with Julie enquiring,

"Shall we head round to Kerasia again today?"

"Why not!" I replied.

We donned light attire, filled our shoulder bag with towels and cossies and trundled off down the road out of Kalami. Unfortunately, ten minutes later Kouloura beckoned us for a coffee. So, not wanting to be rude, we slumped into two chairs with a commanding view of Albania and the mid-morning sun. Kerasia could be seen from our vantage point and sailing would take no more than five minutes. Walking, however, took near on thirty.

Two cappuccinos later we dragged ourselves away from the beauty of Kouloura, up the steep road and down the other side to the beach then picked up the track as it climbs above the cliffs en-route to Kerasia. The path isn't very wide and in some places overhung with branches and foliage, but it was a well-trod path that had probably seen thousands of tourist and local feet alike pass between the bays.

The path eventually drops down steeply and deposits you on to the long, curving beach. A wooden walkway exactly like that of Kalami extends all the way to the taverna at the far end. To the right, the sea and countless loungers; to the left, olive trees and sporadic villas.

We had walked up another thirst so the taverna was the first port of call. As it was nearing lunchtime we ordered something light and ate in the stilted restaurant as it sat close to the water's edge. All sides were open and exposed as the warmth of the sun and briny aroma of the sea wafted through. The waves lapped gently against the outcrop of rock that I had sunbathed on a year earlier and a lone pleasure boat softly embraced the jetty where it was tied, hardly moving. Apart from the odd swimmer lazily meandering across the bay and a brace of children frolicking in the surf, nothing else was moving. That was until a column of bodies could be seen emerging onto the far end of the beach from the coastal track. These weren't your average bay-hoppers or day-trippers; these were serious ramblers complete with walking boots, rucksacks and maps! More and more appeared as a steady line some twenty bodies long made their way purposely up the beach towards the taverna.

Julie and I sat watching this spectacle as they as one body marched closer and closer. Suddenly we were inundated with a horde of German backpackers noisily rearranging the furniture with no regard to other diners or even the taverna owner! Tables were dragged from here, chairs from there until they formed a long table through the middle; leaving the rest of the place looking like a tsunami had passed through. They chatted loudly. They ate even louder. Everybody wanted to talk and everybody wanted to be heard. Their turning up was our cue to leave.

We spent a while tanning ourselves along with the odd dip to cool off, all the time keeping half an eye on a possible invasion of the beach from the German contingent. Fortunately, they finished their repast an hour or so later and the last we saw of them was a blur of boots and rucksacks as they marched as one up the steep road out of Kerasia to conquer pastures and tavernas new.

Suitably rested we retraced the track back to Kouloura then picked up the road back to Kalami where we hit the beach and carried on where we left off in Kerasia.

As this was our last night we thought about dining at the third of the eateries tonight, the Taverna White House. Adjoining and named after the villa next door which was the temporary home of the writer Lawrence Durrell, brother of Gerald, more famously known for his book My Family and Other Animals. The reputation of the taverna lived more off its connection to the White House and Durrell more so than its culinary fare. The entrance to the taverna is accessed from the road down some steps. This allowed you to peruse the interior of the restaurant without having to cross the threshold. This for us was enough. The decor and table coverings more resembled a cafe than a respectable eating establishment. We didn't even get as far as reading the menu at the top of the steps to see what was on offer. We hurriedly retraced our steps as a hopeful waiter caught sight of us and began to beckon us to come and take a seat. We headed towards our usual haunt.

Having feasted we returned to our balcony for our regular night-cap. The quiz night was just getting started in the apartments bar and could be heard quite clearly from where we sat. We were never interested enough to go into the bar to join a team or form one but once the quiz was underway we found ourselves joining in. Initially, as we talked, a certain question would be asked and one of us would nonchalantly throw in the answer mid-sentence. But as time went on conversation dried up and we concentrated on as many questions as possible. When it came time for the answers they were either met with "Yes! Got that one right!" or "Damn!" We weren't alone in this for there were many audible groans and sighs emanating from other balconies around us as other would be egg heads were proved wrong in their attempts.

When all entertainments had finished and the last of the goodbyes had died away, a reassuring hush fell over the bay like a child's security blanket. We poured ourselves one more drink, clinked glasses and raised them to Kalami like an old friend being toasted at a farewell gathering. As indeed this was. But it was an old friend that we made sure we'd never lose contact with.

Chapter 7

Dreams & Drama

The previous year's holiday in Kalami proved pretty uneventful, but this year we were back for a special reason. We were on honeymoon.

We had married the previous Saturday but had to wait until the Friday to fly out. This meant four agonising days back at work until we could start our honeymoon officially. We thought about going somewhere exotic or expensively romantic, but in the end, we knew we loved Kalami and were contented there. We had visions of forking out for some far-flung destination only to be disappointed once we were there – so we opted for what we were happiest with, and that was Corfu. Plus, we argued, we could do one of those other places for our fifth anniversary.

One of my work colleagues, the grounds manager, in fact, was also a devotee of Corfu. So every year saw Ron and his partner Julie fly out to Agios Stephanos on the Northwest side of the island. This time they flew out the same dates as us having attended our wedding reception. We bumped into them at Stansted airport where we swapped phone numbers and made arrangements to meet up at some point. They always hired a car on their hols so they said they'd give us a ring and pop over to see us. Unfortunately, this didn't happen as I'd text Ron (a lot cheaper than phoning!) but then I'd not get a reply for a couple of days by which time we'd made other arrangements. This happened three or four times throughout the holiday and saw us eventually give up. It later transpired that Ron had had major problems with his phone. It wasn't until we bumped into them at Corfu airport on the return that it came to light that theirs wasn't the best holiday they'd had!

    I remembered that during our transfer to Kalami we had passed a coach sitting in the outside lane of the dual carriageway but just assumed it had broken down. Turns out that this was Ron and Julie's coach and that it had knocked an old man off his moped who subsequently died. Ron, being ex-military, ended up taking charge of the incident, moved everybody to the back of the coach then tended to the fatally injured old man. Then, in their second week, a man swimming just offshore from them had a heart attack and drowned. They also heard at Stanstead airport on their return that somebody else had drowned in the sea. That now explained why we'd seen two oblong shaped, coffin-sized boxes being loaded onto a plane next to ours at Corfu airport and some square boxes that obviously contained suitcases!

We were a little disappointed with our apartment this time. The year before, as the apartments were quiet, we were allocated a double room complete with two bathrooms, two bedrooms, a shared kitchen and a large balcony. The two bedrooms proved a godsend for what with Julie's insistence on sleeping with the balcony doors open resulting in me waking up once again covered in mozzie bites, the one night I finally put my foot down saw me sleeping in the other bedroom! Although, before I could actually get to sleep I had to chase dozens of the little buggers that had managed to sneak into my room while we were out round and round the room and squish them before I could retire safe in the knowledge that I should have an undisturbed night and a bite-free face.

Unfortunately, this time we were given a smaller apartment, with a shared balcony. I had a word with Gina on reception and explained that we were on honeymoon and would prefer a bit of privacy, Wink! Wink! Nudge! Nudge! But she explained that unfortunately, unlike when we came last year, this year was fully booked and there was nothing she could do. I tried pleading and considered bribery but in the end, we had to accept this, what else could we do? The first week was ok. The couple were nice and chatty and gave us a few books to read when they left. By contrast, the second couple were odd, to say the least.

They both worked in a mental hospital, but I wasn't convinced they shouldn't have been staying there! He would go out every day with a long-sleeved shirt on buttoned all the way up to the collar, ¾ shorts, sandals, long socks and a sombrero type hat adorned with hanging corks. She would go out in a long dress and hat and they would sit on the beach like this all day, no matter how stifling the heat. When they returned he would not utter a word and would walk past us as if we didn't exist, even though she would stop and talk for ages. Once inside their apartment, they would lock the doors and she would start singing as if rehearsing for the karaoke, although she never entered for it? From our short conversations, we gleaned that for the entire holiday he was only eating omelettes as something he ate on the holiday before had upset his stomach!

That evening we dined with friends we had met the first year of visiting Kalami. We had kept in contact with Jeff & Christine, Adele and Jan. In their last email, it turned out they were flying out for what would be our second week. We had arranged to meet in Thomas's for a get-together and to catch up on the last couple of years. It was a wonderful evening where, totally unexpectedly, they presented us with a fluted vase as a wedding gift. Wine and talk flowed freely and unabated. Laughter rang out from every conversation and Jeff and I became more and more lubricated with copious amounts of red wine. Thomas, as ever the genial host, kept us supplied with many bottles of the sweet, golden nectar that was Kumquat and the sharp but refreshing Lemoncello to round off the evening.

The entertainment didn't stop after we left the taverna.

At around two o'clock in the morning, we were awoken by the drunken ravings of a rabid Scotsman occupying the ground floor of a small villa some 100 yards away. Most of his rantings took place inside but periodically he would venture out of his patio doors to air his grievances to an unseen adversary in the garden. We weren't the only ones disturbed by his antics as many people were out on their balconies watching the spectacle. We couldn't see whether he was alone or hear any other voices but, in a broad Glaswegian accent, he was venting his spleen at some unseen antagonist with the odd piece of flying furniture thrown in, or around, for good measure. Unfortunately only the words that could be discerned were the graphic ones!

"YER !#?!@*! ?*X/?X#!!!"
SMASH!!
"I'LL #!*?@!? DO FOR YOU YER #?!*?#!!!"
CRASH!!
"I NO BE AFRAID OF YOU YER "?X?X?? #!?@*#!! ?????? #@*! ??????? LITTLE #*?!!"
CRUNCH!!
"STINKING ?#*!@!?* @#!?*#!!!"
SPLINTER!!!

His antics had created three differing factions amongst the audience: The first were those shouting obscenities back for being woken in the middle of the night and who were desperate to get back to their slumbers. The second were the 'tut-tutters' who were disgraced at his behaviour but didn't want to get involved. The third were enjoying the debacle and were egging him on for more entertainment. Whether he acknowledged any of this or was even aware of our presence was hard to tell as his gesticulations and furore was omnidirectional. To add to this mayhem a stray dog, obviously intrigued as to what was occurring in his neighbourhood, wandered into the garden. This four-legged intruder now became the Scotsman's enemy manifest. Hardly able to stand he began to lash out at the poor creature like some maniacal goose-stepping John Cleese while at the same time waving his arms around like a demented windmill all the while ranting at the poor pooch in broad Scottish gibberish. Totally wasted on a Greek canine! The dog, in turn, now realising he was under attack, began to snap angrily at the Scotsman's flailing legs who then started back-tracking as he tried to retreat to the safety of his villa but only succeeded in falling backwards over a patio table. The dog, now seeing his chance, instantly bit the prostrate Scot on the foot before running off into the night. His scream was interspersed with more unintelligible profanities and he rose hopping about like Zebedee from the Magic Roundabout. By this time the audience had doubled in size and everybody was in hysterics, but the fun didn't stop there. Drunkenness and hopping do not make good bed-fellows as was proved when he lost his balance, fell backwards in through the patio doors, over the top of a sofa and crashed through a wooden coffee table. The audience as one stood and applauded the scene as if it were a Brian Rix farce. When the cheers and laughter finally died away the Scotsman could be heard quite loudly snoring amid the debris that was once his furniture.

    Entertainment now over we all retired to our own beds safe in the knowledge that he was still alive but out for the count. I mentioned all this to Gina on reception the next morning and asked why nobody had called the police. She looked at me puzzled and said;

"If you had called the police they would have just laughed and put the phone down!"

There are two strange anomalies in Corfu and both concerns toilets.

The first is toilet paper. The Greek plumbing system is unable to cope with too much being flushed down the loo so all soiled paper has to be placed in a bin next to the toilet. I first found out about this when checking up before our first holiday. When I read about it the idea revolted me. Not that I was disgusted by the idea of having to do it, but that some poor bugger has to fish all that used paper out of the bin to get rid of it! Fortunately, every bin has a lid to it and is lined with a plastic bag, making it easier to dispose of but no less unappetising a chore. Surprisingly though, no smell emanates from the receptacle, no matter how full. These are then emptied into a larger bin liner and then taken away and burnt. The first couple of times you forget but there didn't seem to be a problem flushing it away. By the end of the holiday, it becomes second nature. So-much-so in fact that when we returned home, I nearly put the loo paper in the small waste bin we have next to the toilet without thinking! It's not a nice job but one which the Greek people accept without question.

The second is door locks. Or more precisely, the lack of them! We first noticed in the apartment that there was no lock on the bathroom door. Bit of a pain we thought but we just made sure we made each other aware we were "JUST GOING TO THE LOO, DEAR!" The first time in Thomas's I used the toilets there to find also there was no lock on the door. This meant having to cough loudly every time somebody else came into the wash basin area of the toilets. 'A bit of maintenance wouldn't go amiss?' I thought to myself. But we then found out that this lack of bathroom furniture wasn't peculiar to just Kalami. In all the cafés and tavernas that we had frequented from Corfu Town to Kassiopi, from the classiest to the crassest, only one establishment had had a lock on the door. This was also true for the women's. Even at the airport, there are two sets of toilets that must have around 12 cubicles between them in the men's alone, and out of all of them, only one has a lock! Apparently, it's the same in the women's. It seems the Corfiots are either very trusting or not easily embarrassed. Many a time saw me sitting with my leg outstretched and my foot jammed against the door, that's when I could reach it. Other times I'd have to lean forward with my hand at the ready to bar the way if disturbed. If neither of this could be achieved then a hurriedly remembered tune would be was hastily and loudly whistled or much coughing and clearing of throat ensued as a warning that the cubicle was 'in use'.

We got to hear on the grapevine that the White House taverna was on the market. "Wish we had the money!" I remarked to Julie.

"If only!" was the reply.

That evening while talking to Thomas we suggested that he buy it and place Michalis, his head waiter, in charge of it. This was met with much um-ing and er-ing, shrugs of the shoulders and dancing around the subject.

"But it could be a little gold mine!" I carried on. "Refurbished and upgraded with proper management you could then have 2/3's of the beach food-wise."

Still no real interest.

"Or you could get somebody else to buy it for you so your names not involved then place your own people in there?"

Again, much head bobbing and shoulder shrugging. So we left it there while Thomas took our order.

"Such a shame," said Julie.

"I know," I replied. "If run properly it could be as successful as this one."

We spent the rest of the evening looking across at a potential money maker and just wished we were in the position to buy then we could spend the rest of our days here. Oh well, all holidays have their dreams!

As we sat at our favourite table in our favourite taverna in our favourite place, we realised our love for each other was enhanced by the love we had for Kalami. For us, it was the perfect setting for our honeymoon, surrounded by a natural beauty and an ambient tranquillity that wrapped itself around you and became absorbed through every pore. With every breath exhaled you could feel yourself sinking more and more as if your very spirit were permeating through your feet forming a bond that made you one with the spirit of Kalami. The only thing that was missing from this perfection was a full moon for alas, it had come and gone. It had pebbles instead of sand; olive trees instead of palm trees; apartment's en-bloc instead of bungalow's on stilts; but to us, this was our Maldives, our Bahamas, our paradise island.

The next day saw us venture into Kassiopi again and head straight for our favourite café bar, Angevines. This was a two floored affair with a wooden balcony overlooking the harbour shaded by large square parasols. Two cappuccinos were ordered from the owner, an amiable man who wore a welcoming smile and spoke very good English. Unlike many English, the Greeks are always willing to spend time to chat with you regardless of the fact that most oft-asked questions are about the weather. 'How hot is it going to get today?' 'What was the summer like?' 'Does it rain much here?' 'How long will this go on for?' etc, etc. They've heard these same questions time after time, day in day out, dozens of times every day, but they never tire of this and will always answer you with a smile. Our Greek host, Steve, was always happy to supply information and facts about the town or the area or just to tell us about his life.

"When the season finishes," he informed us, "I close up and spend the winter in my place in the hills, hunting and shooting game for my table until the following May comes around then it's back to my bar."

A simple life on a beautiful island.

Julie decided to show me another bay that she and her daughter Becki had found when they had come out for a week in May of last year. The reason for this was that the previous year while sunning ourselves on an early holiday in Gran Canaria, I suddenly announced that I was going to walk the Pennine Way, again! I say again for I had completed it in 1990 after one aborted attempt the previous year and had tried it again about half a dozen times since, all ending in failure. I had always promised myself that I would do it again before I got too old and now seemed good a time as any.

"Are you serious?" said Julie.

"Dead right I am!" I replied.

"How you gonna do it and how long does it take?"

"Two weeks and camping all the way, just like before."

"But you're 53 now; you're not as fit as you were back then?"

"I know," rather hurt by the veiled 'getting on a bit' remark. "But I've got the gym at work and I'll have to lose some weight."

"Up to you Dave!" she replied. "In that case, I'm off to Corfu with Becki for a week!"

Unfortunately, I didn't prepare or train properly for the walk and the morning of the third day saw me on my mobile to Julie.

"You were right luv, I'm totally unfit. I'm calling it a day."

"Never mind," she said. "What you gonna do now?"

"Get myself back home and try and get a flight out to you for the rest of the week if I can."

This proved to be financially impossible as there were no package holidays available and flights were so expensive I could have bought Corfu for less!

We walked out of Kassiopi and turned left down a small road then turned off down a small track that led to three old houses, the end one of which was uninhabited and in much need of repair. Rounding the side of the house we came across Avlaki beach, a long pebbly shore backed onto by a handful of private villas. It was a totally deserted stretch of beach that swept round in a large horseshoe bay. The abandoned house was a two storey affair. It was built into a rise, that is, the ground at the front of the house was higher than the back, this meant the front door opened onto the upper floor and, from the front, looked to be just a single storey. On the beach side, the upper floor had a few shuttered windows and the lower floor had two larger openings, boarded over. The once painted walls were now faded and weathered, the roof sagged in places and the end wall showed large cracks, a result of subsidence and neglect. But we saw potential. We pictured it as a taverna and bar. The top floor would be the drinking area and the lower would be more open with tables spilling out onto the surrounding area of grass where a mixture of Greek and English food would be served. All would be exposed timber work and wooden floors with subdued lighting and soft music. Those lucky enough to have an outside table would dine to the sounds of the gentle lapping waves on the pebbles and the distant glow of lights of Albania. Yes, it was out of the way but new apartments had been built just a few hundred yards back up the road from which we came. We even had a name for it already. 'Shirley's Place'. In the film Shirley Valentine, all she ever wanted to do was to drink authentic Greek wine while sitting by the water's edge. Well, here she could do that!

"What do you think?" I enquired of Julie.

"Gorgeous," she replied. "But we have neither the funds or time to be able to do it. Plus, we don't know who owns it or why it's abandoned?"

I knew she was talking sense, but for a short while, we nearly had our reason not to go home.

As it was such a lovely, warm day, and we were in no rush, we decided to walk back to Kalami. We weren't sure how far it was or how long it would take but we went for it anyway. We followed the beach for about 1000mts where we picked up a narrow road that led in the right direction. We followed this as it wound on and ever upwards until finally reaching a T junction. The sea was in front and far below us. If we turned right we would be walking further inland but perhaps towards a main road. Turn left and the road descended windingly towards Agios Stefanos. We opted for the latter in the hope that the road continued out the other side.

The walk down was steep in places and long in time, mainly because of the many stoppages to take in the fantastic views that could be had from the high vantage points. Cobalt seas, azure skies, glacier white yachts and a multitude of greens could be observed for miles. The distant Corfu town shimmered in the heat haze like a desert mirage. Down below us Agios Stefanos, a tiny hamlet of whitewashed abodes nestled around a secluded bay. We were caught between a desire to stay and drink in the vista and the longing to experience the delights of the harbour. When we finally descended the long and winding road (I feel a song coming on), we were hot, sweaty and tired but a couple of drinks and a sit down by the harbour soon paid to that.

Agios Stefanos

The bay itself hosted four tavernas, a few mini-markets and numerous villas and apartments. It is a favourite of the English and many Brits live here permanently giving rise to its nickname 'Kensington-on-Sea'. Everything about the place was inviting, the waters, the tavernas lining the harbour edge, the whitewashed villas, the calm shingle beach, the quietude. It was a perfect idyll in a perfect setting. We were loath to leave but leave we must for we knew not how much further there was to go.

    The road rose as it left the harbour, feeling steeper than it actually was due in part to our tiredness. Soon it was dropping again and we followed a wall to our left that surrounded a huge, private estate. It suddenly dawned on us as the next bay came into view that we were nearing Kerasia and that this was the estate of the Rothschild dynasty. We were now in familiar territory. Kalami was now just 45minutes away so we could afford to stop for a longer rest and a long, cold drink. Fortunately, the taverna was Germans free this time so the rest was peaceful and uninterrupted, to a point!
    A well-spoken but slightly inebriated Englishman who spoke fluent Greek was holding court with the taverna owners. 'Was this one of the Rothschild's?' I wondered. 'Should I buy him a drink?' was the next thought, thinking this would

guarantee an invite to his next soiree! Instead, we just sat and watched his antics, his wild gesticulations as he babbled on incoherently (to us anyway) in his Anglo-Greek dialect. The taverna owners, sometimes grinning, sometimes laughing, went about their business taking it in turns to keep the conversation going. But, not being able to understand Greek, perhaps they were laughing at his words, not at his condition. We couldn't tell.

Rested and watered, we finally left the retreat and headed off along the beach to pick up the high coastal track that would take us back to Kalami. Even from the other end of the shore, we could still hear him as clear as day.

We first noticed them as a couple the day before but now he was sitting on his own at in Thomas's at lunchtime looking slightly forlorn. As usual, Julie decided to befriend him.

"Where's your wife today?"

"She's not feeling too well, decided to stay in the villa," he replied in a defined Welsh accent.

"Come and join us if you want," I suggested.

"Don't mind if I do!" he said, looking rather happy at the invitation.

"I'm Dave and this is Julie."

"I'm Ray and my wife, when she emerges, is Maureen."

"Been out here long?" I asked.

"This is our second week," he replied.

"Same here," we said. "But it's a bit different for us. We're on honeymoon." I added.

"Congratulations!" he said as he shook my hand and kissed Julie on the cheek.

We ordered coffees for ourselves and a whiskey for Ray. We learnt that he and his wife were retired army officers in the medical corps. Ray had been a captain and his wife a major. They were also parish councillors for their local village, a role he seemed to relish since leaving the army. He was of a smallish statue, thin with a wisp of hair draped across his head Bobby Charlton style. She was only an inch or two taller, slightly rounded but 'sturdier' than he. He looked nothing like a captain; she looked every part the major!

"Beautiful place to come for a honeymoon," he observed.

"I know. W.e could have gone anywhere else but there's some special about Kalami" said Julie.

"You can say that again? Been coming here for quite a few years now. There's no place like it." said Ray. "We were here in the late '90s when the war was going on in Albania. You could sit here all day and watch the Greek destroyers sailing back and forth patrolling the waters. Bit scary really."

"You're parish councillors as well. What does that entail?"

"Stirring things up at council meetings!" he said with a sparkle in his eye. "They're a bit namby-pamby when it comes to organisation, so we tend to take over. They think a lot of our recommendations are controversial but we don't care, it keeps them on their toes!"

Our conversation jumped from subject to subject. The state of the NHS, decline in morals, crime, education, youth, the welfare state etc, before he struck us both dumb when he suddenly stated quite loudly;-

"I tell you what's wrong with our country; it's all the bloody blacks and the gays!!"

Julie & I looked at each other incredulously. We'd only just met him and he had no idea what our beliefs or standing was on such matters but here he was, airing his views to the world regardless of offence. We made allowances for this as he had consumed quite a few shots of whiskey at this point and was starting to look a little worse for wear. We looked round to see if anybody else had been within listening distance. If they had, nobody showed it.

As controversial as his comments were, he was still a likeable chap. The following day we met Maureen who had gotten over her bout of sickness. She was quite a formidable woman and definitely wore the trousers in the relationship. Not only did she outrank him in the army, she outranked him in the marriage as well. She was just as outspoken as Ray and we could imagine them as quite a fearsome brace of parish councillors. She did admit that they tried to put the fear of God into the others when they wanted things done their way.

She also related to us that a friend of theirs that was out here on holiday once with them suffered a heart attack and was taken to the main hospital in Corfu Town. She went to visit him later that day and was disgusted at the state of the intensive care unit that she described as no better than a sluice room! She immediately tore into the doctors, the nurses and holiday rep. Next day he was transferred to a private hospital. Such was the power, or scariness, of the woman.

As usual, our holiday/honeymoon was over before it had begun. The previous evening we had been presented with a small gift set from Alexandra, a bottle of wine from Thomas and hugs all round. As usual, Julie welled up at the thought of having to leave in the morning which resulted in more hugs from Alexandra.

"I'm a bit worried this bottle might push my suitcase up over the weight limit?" I said to Julie the next morning.

"Carry it then," she replied.

"But won't they stop me going through customs?"

"Shouldn't do? When Becki and I went to Hanioti some years ago they allowed us to take drink through!"

I should have known? When we tried to pass through customs I was stopped and told to drop the bottle in their bin.

"It's a present from a taverna owner!" I said

"You cannot take it through, put it in the bin." came the reply

"But it was given especially as a wedding present, I didn't buy it!" I reasoned.

"Not allowed through, please put it in the bin!"

"But, we got it from Thomas, at Kalami!" for some reason thinking they would know him?

"It's not allowed, please put it in the bin, SIR!"

The 'sir' bit did the trick. You knew they were getting serious when they used 'sir'. I did as I was told and had to be content with buying a bottle of the same wine in duty-free, some six feet away from where the officers were standing!

That was the only downer to the honeymoon, everything else, the weather, the friends, the hospitality, the welcome, the scenery, the location, the tranquillity, the slow pace etc, etc, were perfection itself. Yes, we could have been enjoying soft white sands, all-inclusive service, our own hut on stilts perched over blue waters in some far-flung exotic location like the Maldives or the Bahamas, but we didn't want it. Our little bit of heaven was right here – and we couldn't wait to come back.

> STANDARDS AT
> CONCERNING
> OF DISABLED
> PERSONS WITH

Sign above disabled seating in Corfu airport.

Chapter 8

Damp days & Dirty dogs

We were not alone this year. When Julie was growing up, her mum's cousin, Richard, and she were very close, almost like brother and sister, even though there was an eight-year age gap between them. This relationship had never waned and both have been very supportive of the other through troubled times. Over the years though, Richard had suffered with continuing ill health which made holidaying a hit and miss affair and sometimes restrictive. With a lull in his treatment, he and his wife Karen were looking for somewhere to go at the end of September. I checked our operator and found there were still places left at the A&A apartments, so we invited them to come away with us for our week in Corfu. They both jumped at the proposal.

They drove up from Dorset on Thursday staying at ours for the early morning push off. As sad as it sounds Julie and I always watched Shirley Valentine just before our holiday, just to get us in the mood. Tonight was no exception.

Unfortunately, this time Richard and Karen had to suffer our little foible. I suppose it's the equivalent of having to sit through other people's umpteen holiday slides, but in reverse!

As usual, we were at the airport three hours before the flight departed where we perused the now familiar duty-free outlets. We knew these like the backs of our hands now, having frequented them every year for the past six years. After a spot of light breakfast and coffees that killed about 40minutes, we were at a loss for something to do so, once again, we paraded round and round the shops just to kill time. Passing an ATM Richard decided to draw some more money out, in case of emergencies. He inserted his card then watched in disbelief as it swallowed the piece of plastic willingly but refused to issue any money. There was not even a notice that popped up to say 'Contact your bank' that would give some indication of the problem. We all stood scratching our heads as to what to do next.

"Well, somebody must have a key to open these things up?" suggested Julie.

"Good idea," said Richard. "Problem is where do we find them at 4 o'clock in the morning?"

I suggested the bureau de change might have access to them, they being involved in all things monetary. Richard approached their desk but was duly informed that nobody had access to the machines accept the men that refilled them, and that wasn't gonna happen at this time of the day! While that was happening we stood guard over the machine, turning away people who approached to save them the same fate. Through the wonders of technology, I was able to access the website of his bank on my phone and find the number for credit card enquiries. One phone call later and his card was cancelled and another issued to be waiting at home on his return. Thank God for 24hr help desks! This wasn't a good start to the holiday.

It was unusual to find Thomas in his taverna on a Friday afternoon. But here he was, as amiable as ever. Hugs and kisses were exchanged with him and Alexandra, and Karen and Richard were introduced. They were greeted like old friends; such is the warmth of the Corfiots.

"Table 16 tonight?" enquired Thomas, not forgetting.

"Definitely, but for four please," I replied.

"Of course, I will join two together."

Before long, we were ensconced on four loungers in front of his eatery where our rat-race mentality was replaced with the calmer 'it can wait till tomorrow' mindset. Hardly a word was spoken, nothing needed to be said. The surroundings, the ambience, the seascape said it all. After some time Richard exclaimed,

"I can see why you keep coming back here."

"Beautiful isn't it?" replied Julie.

We dined together that night where I introduced Richard to the delights of Tiropitakia and lamb hotpot. Karen and Julie opted for fish. We were served by Vlad who had been with Thomas for about four years now but who we knew well from our subsequent visits.

"Kalispera Dave. Kalispera Julie!" he said with a wide grin.

"Kalispera Vlad. How are you, my friend?" I enquired.

"I'm good. Good to see you back again."

"You know us, Vlad, we can't keep away."

I introduced Richard and Karen to him.

"Kalispera!" he bade them with a warm smile.

Richard looked confused.

"It means good evening," I explained.

He didn't try to repeat it, just said 'Hi' instead.

"Half red for you Dave, and half white for you Julie?" Vlad enquired, knowing our drinking habits from before.

"Make it a litre of white Vlad and a bottle of water please."

"Of course. Efharisto."

Richard didn't drink but the girls both liked white. I could have ordered a litre of red for myself but I don't think I'd have made it back up the 200 or steps back to our apartment. The repast was eaten amid stories recounted of long-ago childhood memories when Richard and Julie were growing up together. Laughter and happiness reigned that evening. Then, in the black inkiness of night, a glowing, silent vessel of steel and light slowly hove into view as it rounded the headland to our right. All stopped and gazed as the luminescent gargantuan, ablaze with lights from forecastle to aft, cut through the waters soundless except for the low hum of its engines. I doubt if there wasn't a single person sitting there that didn't wish they were aboard the craft at that precise moment. But, as Julie commented, the passengers on the liner may well have been looking at us and wishing they were dining in a taverna on the beach?

There was something different about the White House taverna. It's raised dining area was bathed in subdued lighting and had a cosier feel about it. To the seaside of the taverna, a few steps down from the main eating area was a flat, rocky outcrop that sat a few inches above the water which sported a jetty, alighting those in small dinghy's that had rowed ashore from more grandiose yachts and catamarans anchored in the bay. A few candlelit tables now adorned this shelf of rock lending itself a more romantic air. It definitely had more of an inviting look about it now.

"We must check it out sometime?" I said to Julie.

"Have you noticed the absence of Michalis?" she said, half asking, half stating.

"Yes. You're not thinking what I am, are you? I replied.

"We'll definitely have to check it out!" she said.

Richard and Karen looked at us quizzically.

The first couple of days were spent idly on the beach, returning back to our apartment for lunch as eating in the tavernas twice a day was proving expensive. This was due to the falling value of the Euro against the pound, resulting in getting less when changing up our money. When we first went to Corfu we used to get €1.33 to £1, now we were only getting €1.13. Doesn't sound a lot but on £500 that means a difference of €100 less for the week. By eating in our apartment, just a light salad, we actually managed to save nearly £200.

Sunday night was Greek night and, although we'd seen it every time we'd been, it was a first for

Richard and Karen. We made sure we'd finished our meal at Thomas's by nine so we could be in time to grab a table in the Cocktail & Dreams bar. There were always four men and two women who performed the variety of dances, two of the men dressed in white shirts and black trousers, the other two all in black. The woman wore a black skirt, white blouse with a red sash round her waist. The first few dances involved the white-shirted men and the woman and mainly consisted of all three linking arms and either dancing round in circles or straight line charges from one end to the other. Occasionally, one of the men would kick his legs up as high as he could go and then slap his foot with his hand. We could not work out the significance of this, maybe it was a traditional Greek courtship dance to show how fit and supple the male suitor was! The woman just danced around with a hanky and a smile? Then there came what looked like the dance of the macho men.

    The white-shirted and black-shirted dancers took up positions either end of the patio area where tin trays were filled with a flammable liquid and ignited. The two separate sets of 'opponents' then linked arms and repeatedly charged at each other. Once one pair reached the other end the other pair would then push them back. As with the other dances, there was a lot of high leg kicking thrown in but this was probably to show who was fitter and stronger rather than as a courtship ritual, but I could be wrong!

Then came a familiar piece of music that anybody outside Greece knows, Zorbas dance! As soon as the music started everybody involuntarily began to clap in time and sway to the rhythm. This was accompanied by washing up bottles filled with the same flammable liquid as before being squirted onto the patio floor. Initially, it looked like just a random pattern but once lit the flames spelt out ZORBA to amazed gasps from the crowd. We'd seen it before so we just acted nonplussed, although I was always fascinated by this and couldn't wait for this bit! The dancing then started in earnest with the black-clad artistes coming into their own. Much WHOOPA!, high kicking and spinning movements were woven amongst rivulets of flame spreading out across the floor from enthusiastic squirter's adding a touch of danger and excitement to the dance. Many a time blue flames licked across their shoes and trouser bottoms but these were quickly extinguished from the nifty footwork of the dancers.

Then came the chance for everybody to join in and make a fool of themselves. But with copious amounts of Ouzo, Retsina and beer flowing like water, who cared! The dancers weaved in and out of the tables hauling people up to join in the Greek version of the conga. Richard, Karen and Julie were two of those picked to join 30 or 40 other people in a 'train' that wove round the patio area, in and out of the tables, around the swimming pool before returning to the start where they were then had to weave under the arms of those at the back without breaking hold. Eventually, the 'train' became tighter and tighter from all the weaving and ended in a complete standstill and much laughter. I was pleased I managed to escape being chosen as I was, very timely, getting another round of drinks in. Unfortunately, I was targeted as I returned to the table.

My derrière had hardly touched the seat before one of the white-shirted dancers grabbed hold of my arm, dragged me out into the middle and indicated to me to follow his lead. People were clapping and whooping like those annoying; overexcited audiences, you get on live American TV shows. He executed a few simple leg movements to get some measure of me. I emulated these with ease. He then stepped up a gear and made the movements a little more complicated. Again, I copied them pretty closely, much to the admiration of the audience. I began to feel quite chuffed at my achievements so far. I was no dancer but I was holding my own. Sensing a bit of competition he decided to go for height. He threw a few head high kicks in the air and, with a look that said 'Try those then cocky!' he beckoned me to follow. The audience also turned to look at me but with incredulous hope. But I had an ace up my sleeve. Unbeknown to him, many years ago I used to teach Kung Fu so high kicking was not alien to me. To gasps and cheers from the onlookers and with my old joints being copiously lubricated with red wine I copied him kick for kick and height for height. I'd upped the ante! We could both feel the tide of admiration was now turning in my favour, but he wasn't gonna be beaten. He next launched into a very complicated and involved routine of high kicks, twists, foot slapping and dips that seemed to go on and on. When finished he stood sweating and somewhat breathless in front of me, hands on hips, waiting. I could feel the crowd looking at me expectantly. We stood like two gunslingers, waiting to see who would be the first to draw or back down. I held his gaze as rivulets of sweat ran down my face and back. My feet and hands twitched as a slight smirk crossed his face. My fans waited eagerly. Suddenly I launched into the famous Morecambe and Wise skipping dance that they performed while singing 'Bring me Sunshine' at the end of their shows. This received a rapturous applause from the audience, a huge grin from my adversary and saved us both a loss of face.

"Same old faces!"

We looked up to see the broadly smiling visages of Jeff and Christine.

"Hi-Ya!" We said in unison as we rose from our loungers.

We embraced them like long lost friends.

"Great to see you again! When did you get here? How long you here for?" we enquired.

"Got here yesterday and here for two weeks," replied Christine. "And you?"

"Just a week unfortunately," replied Julie. "By the way, this is Richard my cousin, and his wife Karen, they're out here with us this year."

Handshakes and hugs ensued.

"Where's Jan and Adele?" I enquired.

"Back at the apartment. Where are you eating tonight?"

"Thomas's. Joining us?" Julie asked.

"No, we're eating at the White House tonight. Why don't you join us?" Jeff asked.

Julie looked at me, then Richard and Karen. We all shrugged our shoulders and said: "Why not!"

"It's a date then!" said Jeff. "OK, see you at 8 then. We're just off to Kouloura for lunch, catch you later."

We resumed our positions and carried on where we left off. Julie began to feel a little guilty as the loungers outside the taverna now belonged to Thomas, as opposed to the little Greek lady who seemed to own the whole beach.

"Do you think we should move?" She said.

"Why?"

"Because we're using his loungers but we're not eating in his taverna tonight."

"Yeah, but just think of how many times we do use it. We have a coffee there first thing in the morning and eat there most nights." I replied.

"Fair enough!" she said and turned over.

We arrived at 7.45 to be greeted by a young blonde woman who, surprisingly, wasn't Greek. We were immediately beckoned over to a large table already occupied by Jeff and the others. More hugs, more kisses, more handshakes ensued. Richard and Karen were introduced more informally this time and were at complete ease by the time drinks were ordered. Menus were perused but it didn't take long for Richard and me to make up our minds. Kleftico! As we waited for the others to decide what they were having a familiar voice spoke from behind asking if we were ready to order.

"Michalis!" I said, rising to welcome him.

"How are you darling?" said Julie as she gave him a hug.

"I'm good, very good. And you?"

"It's Kalami, how would we be?" I replied.

"So, Thomas took our advice and bought this place and put you in charge then?" I shot Julie a glance.

"No! No! No!" he replied hurriedly. "I only work here. It is owned by Tassos!"

He looked awkward at being asked.

"Then why did you leave Thomas?" I carried on.

"Money better," he said with a grin. The same grin that he always had.

"Well, it's great to see you again," I said.

"And you my friend," he replied and meant it.

We sat back down shooting sideways glances at each other and nodding knowingly. With Thomas having his taverna, the gift and the travel shop; his brother Dimitrie with his taverna and a horse riding centre; it seemed everything and everyone around here had some sort of connection to each other in some way or another. The Greeks have a habit of keeping a lot of businesses within the family, not just fathers and brothers; theirs extends to first, second and third cousins, distant uncles, long lost aunties, disowned grandchildren and the odd goat!

The evening wore on but never dulled. Conversations criss-crossed the table, alternating from person to person and subject to subject. Richard and Jeff got on like the proverbial burning abode. Julie and Karen were lost in their tête-àtête. Myself, Christine, Jan and Adele were immersed in a conversation about ghosts and things spiritual! How we ever got onto that subject I'll never know but alcohol probably played a major part.

It was gone midnight when we realised we were the only ones left in the taverna. Michalis and others were busy clearing up from the evening's guests and readying the tables for the morning. Alas, when the festivities are over the guests must depart. We did this as the rain began to fall gently on Kalami. By the time we'd climbed the steps to the road Michalis had turned up with a people carrier.

"What's this for?" I enquired.

"Please, get in," replied Michalis. "It is raining, I drive you back to your apartments."

"But it's not far Michalis, we can walk and it's only rain!"

"No, please!" he wouldn't be deterred. "I run you back."

We felt we'd hurt his feelings if we declined so we climbed in and he ran us the 500mts back to the apartments, even driving right up to the entrance to the lifts so we didn't have to walk the last 50mts in the rain! Was there no end to Greek hospitality?

The White House

Five days in Richard and Karen said they'd like to visit Corfu town and, as the weather report for the day was extensive cloud, we decided to go with them. We caught the bus at the top of the road above Kalami and within five minutes the heavens opened. Twice, the downpour was so heavy the bus had to stop as visibility was practically zero. Obviously, there was a limit even to devil-may-care Greek drivers. When we finally pulled into the bus terminus it had eased a little but a torrent of water was cascading down the road which fed into the upper exit of the depot and ran like a river through it and out of the lower exit on to the harbour carriageway. Fortunately, we were all wearing flip-flops so we made a dash through the deluge to the terminus café. Once inside we wished we hadn't. The term greasy spoon didn't do it justice. Everything was greasy! The decor had seen better days, so to the food. We stuck to just having a coffee when we eventually got served that is! While the coffee cooled I decided to spend a penny. Shame they hadn't spent a few pennies on revamping the toilets! There was no urinal, just a pan and surprise, surprise, no lock on the door! I'm glad I didn't have to sit down for there was no seat either and looked like it hadn't been cleaned since the day it was installed. The door was to one side so I had to stand with my right foot jammed up against it while trying to aim into the bowl, hoping I had enough force to reach it. Initially, this was successful but as my bladder became more and more depleted I found myself having to edge closer and closer to the pan. With the state of the floor I needn't have bothered but, by God, I'm English! Eventually, my stance became so wide that I was close to doing the splits before being fully relieved. I left the cubicle, washed my hands in cold water and looked for a towel. Why I should have thought there was going to be a towel in here I've got no idea so I had to depart the toilets with my dripping hands held up in front of me like a surgeon waiting for a nurse to dress him with surgical gloves. I eventually wiped them on my shorts as I reasoned they couldn't get any wetter!

Coffees drunk we ventured out of the terminus and headed up the road against the flow of the river. The rain had subsided a little but was still constant. Such was the resourcefulness of the Greek people that there were already entrepreneurs on every street selling umbrellas. It boded the question, where the hell did they get all these umbrellas at such short notice? I'm pretty sure that if it was to snow they'd be out there with snow shovels! Or, if there was a heat wave, they'd appear with parasols! With no sign of abatement, we purchased two umbrellas from one vendor and headed off into the heart of the town. We negotiated familiar streets and back alleys before emerging into a small square where a homely looking taverna took our fancy. A moustachioed gentleman wiping down a table outside beckoned us in perfect English. He had a rugged Greek look about him but sounded more like an east London café owner. We were shown to a table and it wasn't until Julie sat down that she realised her knickers were wet! She was met with the usual juvenile comments from Richard and me.

"Couldn't wait for the toilet?" ha, ha.

"Can't hold it in anymore?" he, he.

"Had too much to drink have we?" guffaw, guffaw.

The answer was less embarrassing. The gipsy skirt Julie was wearing had a liner and in the course of walking the sodden streets, the water had been soaked up by the liner, all the way up to her underwear! Now sitting, it was uncomfortably cold and caused her to squirm in her seat. A quick visit to the toilet enabled her to wring some of the water out, not resolving the problem but at least making it more bearable.

Julie and I just had a light lunch while Richard and Karen ordered home-made burgers. These took a little while to come and we had practically finished ours by then, but the reason became obvious when they were finally served. These weren't the type of burgers that are served in those cheap, plastic decored, cooked in ten seconds, tastes of cardboard outlets; these were thick, succulent, 100% beef slabs of meat on freshly baked buns. I was slavering at the aroma and meatiness for these were a feast in themselves. No garnish or chips, just pure, unadorned, ½ pound, wholesome beef burgers. They took an age to devour, but we weren't in a hurry.

When we did finally emerge the rain had been replaced by the more familiar blue skies and golden sunshine. Vapour rose from the pavements as the heat from the sun condensed any rain still lying on the paths and roads. Life returned to the back streets, deserted from the onset of the deluge. Goods appeared back outside shops again. Lacework, clothing, wooden crafts, postcards, religious paraphernalia, tourist junk, lotions, sunglasses, newspapers etc. As quickly as they had been dragged inside they were hurriedly laid out again.

Shops perused, sights seen, cafés haunted and streets trudged, we all made our way back to the terminus, found our bus and made the hour return journey to Kalami, noticing new sights we hadn't we hadn't seen in our umpteen trips prior. What we also noticed was a lot more empty cafés and shops. Lean times were starting to hit Corfu.

"Fancy Kassiopi this afternoon?" We enquired of Richard and Karen in the morning.

"Whatever you suggest?" replied Richard. "Is it far?"

"Just 15 minutes by bus. It's a lovely harbour town, nothing like Kalami."

"Fine by us!" he said, both nodding.

The mid-afternoon bus deposited us at the small market square. Here, locals and tourists alike took advantage of the shade offered by a large tree in the middle of the square. With temperatures around 30c, it was a welcome respite. We sauntered along the road that led down to the harbour passing the local junior school where young Cretan children were being disciplined in the art of traditional Greek dancing in the playground. To our right, the entrance to a small church. Next door, a clothes shop selling all the tourist paraphernalia you could wish for, mainly T-shirts with rude, sometimes near pornographic, inscriptions. Further along, an old lady sat in her shop crocheting a babies shawl. Cotton ware of all descriptions filled her shelves and hung from every spare inch of space, all painstakingly and lovingly woven as she sat day-by-day, week after week in her little shop, hoping for custom. The road swept down and around to the right where it opened up onto the harbour front. At one time, between the tavernas and the quayside, there used to be a car park area; now, a large, raised grassed island has taken its place with just a few parking spaces and a one-way system, which all of the locals ignored.

We headed as usual for our favourite café bar, climbed the stairs and plonked ourselves into the thickly padded, wicker chairs sat under large umbrellas. We were welcomed by Steve who recognised us immediately from our numerous prior visits over the years.

"Welcome my friends. You have brought guests this time!"

"Hi-Ya," we replied.

"This is my cousin and his wife," said Julie.

"Welcome. Your first time to Corfu?" he enquired.

"Yes, but won't be our last," replied Richard. "It's beautiful here."

"That it is my friend. That it is. What can I get you, please?"

"Four cappuccinos, parakalo. Efharisto"

I felt like a native now, speaking fluent Greek. Well, I could say please and thank you anyway!

We all sat and watched life pass us by from the balcony. Occasionally, a tourist bus would drive down to the harbour and deposit a hoard of sightseers onto the waterfront. This caused mayhem for traffic behind the coach and for those trying to get out of the harbour. The road was wide enough for two cars to pass but the coach, being wider and longer, unintentionally blocked the bend and therefore the harbour entrance. Once deposited, there then came the fiasco of the coach then having to try and reverse up a small road to the left so it could then swing round and drive back up round the bend where it would park itself a few hundred yards up the main road in a proper car park. Why it didn't do this in the first place and let the passengers walk down I'll never know?

A small flotilla of hire boats were tied up along the front. A couple of large passenger boats, slowly filling with sightseeing day-trippers, were moored in prime central positions. The concrete jetty was adorned with half-a-dozen yachts of various sizes bearing flags of differing nationalities. Between us and Albania, ferries and liners swept noiselessly back and forth. The tavernas, both on the quayside and those setback, were struggling for custom.

We sat, we talked, we coffee'd more. Why rush? Corfu didn't!

As we sat people watching we noticed a German couple having problems with their motor yacht. He had climbed on board and fired up the engine while she untied the mooring ropes in the hope of following him. Unfortunately, the motor that hauled up the anchor refused to do its job. She waited patiently on the quayside while he tried time and time again to get the thing working, but to no avail. Eventually, the Greek owner of the small hire boats came to his aid. Between them, they kicked and thumped, tugged and wrenched and swore constantly. We assumed it was swearing as, although in German and Greek, the words had the same venom and articulation as English swear words. All this time the wife just stood there, still holding the rope as if her life depended on it. After nearly 20mins of coaxing the motor finally kicked in and the anchor chain began to tighten. As it did so the yacht began to be drawn forwards as the anchor had been dropped some 30ft away. So overjoyed were the two sailors that they'd eventually sorted out the problem that they totally forgot the wife, who was still holding the rope! As the boat crept forever forward this slipped gradually through her hands until she realised it was running out. Then, for some unknown reason, she tried desperately to hold on to the remainder? Whether she thought that by doing so she could stop the boat going too far is any bodies guess? Time and time again she was pulled forward to the harbours edge, just letting go at the last second before dropping back and grabbing another handful before being pulled forward again. Then she had the idea that she should run around the edge of the harbour, still holding the rope, and try and catch up with the yacht!

We all sat there, mouths open saying "For God's sake, let go of the rope you stupid woman!" Fortunately, a passing tourist who, like us, had been watching the events unfold, just managed to grab hold of her as she came to the end of the line and was being pulled to the quays edge and into the water. Her husband was totally oblivious to all this and only realised she wasn't on board when she suddenly appeared at the end of the jetty by the harbour entrance waving frantically.

Greek alighted. Frau boarded. Entertainment over.

"Fancy a walk around the coast road?" I suggested.

"How far does it go?" asked Karen, obviously worried that it may be too far for Richard.

"It actually comes out at the other end of town where we can walk back along the main road and check out some other shops. There's a taverna at the end so we can always stop for a rest if need be." I offered.

"Sounds good to me," said Richard.

The sun had begun its descent for some time now but there was still enough for a good walk. We rounded the quayside and passed the three tavernas that clung to the harbours edge. We veered off momentarily along the jetty to admire the yachts anchored there. A couple were very modern and sleek, looking more like racing yachts then pleasure craft. The others looked more sedate and homely if you can describe a ship as homely? We continued our way up the coast road passing a handful of villas for rent on our left and a sheer drop into the ocean on our right. Thankfully a handrail ensured we didn't. We followed a crazy paving footpath that ran alongside the one-way road until we came upon a lone taverna overlooking Kassiopi beach. This was similar to Kalami beach, as in being pebbly, but on a much smaller scale. There were actually two beaches, split by a rocky promontory, popular with divers. The way down was steep and unsure underfoot, so we didn't bother. Carrying on round, some more private villas were to be found but these were actually sited on the rocky outcrops above the sea, giving uninterrupted views across the Ionian to Albania. These also were for rent but looked expensive, having their own swimming pools, barbeque areas, gardens and large patios adorned with classy looking patio furniture. Obviously, they were fed up with people like us as high fences were being constructed to stop sightseers, or more to the point, nosey parkers! We stopped drooling and pushed on as the road dipped down and veered towards its termination. Here, to our right, another beach, much larger than the other two but less densely populated. To our left, a mixture of villas and apartments lined the road. Some had seen better days. Most were empty.

    We reached the end of the road where an automatic barrier allowed vehicles to exit on the main road. Here too was the last taverna out of Kassiopi. It occupied a prime position that enjoyed unprecedented views of the sun as it sunk into the west. Unfortunately, it was having a day off as it was closed! We headed slowly back into town, passing odd shops and bars. One that always drew our attention was a shop that sold goods and artefacts made out of olive wood. These ranged from pencils to three foot high lizards, delicately and precisely carved and gaily coloured. Every inch of shop space was filled with cleverly turned or chiselled objet d'art. The wood was a mixture of differing browns, highlighted all the more so by being highly polished. By the following year, the shop would be closed.

By the time we returned to the harbour, the sun had set proper and feasting time was upon us. We opted for the Three Brothers taverna where we had the choice of any table as we were the only ones there! The girls chose fish but Richard and I went straight for the Kleftico. As usual, copious amounts of wine, red & white, accompanied the repast. Richards dinner was first to turn up and, unusually, was wrapped in what appeared to be extremely thin filo pastry. He was having trouble trying to cut through it when a passing waitress spotted him and came over and said "Allow me sir", then unwrapped the greaseproof paper to expose the lamb dish beneath it! To his embarrassment, he was met with roars of laughter when we realised what he'd been trying to do. And, just to make sure he never lived it down, it was brought up at practically every meal after that.

It was at this point that we noticed a family; mum, dad and two kids; enter the still deserted taverna. They occupied a table just off to the side of us and sat for ages carefully scrutinising the menu. They eventually gave the waitress what seemed to be a very quick order. As we sat eating our deserts their meal was delivered, but it seemed as if only one dish had turned up, plus one bottle of water? As we watched we were gobsmacked to watch all four of them huddled round, sharing the one meal and the bottle of water! Either they were tight or skint!

As we ate and gazed out across the harbour to the darkening shores of Albania our pity suddenly fell on a small, three-legged dog that hobbled across the quayside. There always seemed to be dogs wandering about in Kassiopi, none of them attached to an owner. They were never a nuisance and there never seemed to be any evidence of their comings and goings. They just did what dogs do, namely smell each other's butts! Not so with this little tri-limbed lothario. He was way beyond the introductions stage of mutual butt odour appreciation. But, what he lacked in limbs he made up for in libido and every canine, regardless of size or gender, was fair game. Every passing pooch, whether they wanted to or not, suddenly found themselves rogered senseless by this randy little cur. His stamina was amazing. No sooner had he dismounted, or more likely the poor recipient managed to escape, then he had waylaid another. There was nothing stopping this canine Casanova, and all this with only one back leg!

This went on continually for the next hour or so and nothing escaped his amorous advances. Even the feline population wasn't safe! He eventually ran out of conquests and disappeared, or so we thought? All of a sudden a cry went out and the table went up from the frugal family next to us and we turned to see the woman frantically thrashing about screaming "Get it off!" "GET IT OFF!" We wondered what the cause of this mayhem was when we suddenly saw our three-legged friends happily humping the hell out of her leg! More tables and chairs went flying as she tried desperately to loosen his tight grip on her leg by shaking it wildly. This only resulted in the horny hound getting more and more excited. Eyes now bulging and panting wildly, the more she shook her leg, the more the dog tightened its grip, enjoying the ride. Her husband aimed wild kicks at the mutt, missing every time as the wife wouldn't stand still long enough for him to take proper aim. The kids were in hysterics as they watched their mum hopping around the taverna on one leg screaming while a deranged dog made wild passionate love to the other. We were laughing too much to be of any assistance and were much happier to sit and watch the entertainment.

Eventually, with the aid of a bucket of water and a broom, the loved-up lapdog was prised off her leg and was chased out of the taverna and up the road. We had the hardest job to stifle our amusement as she stood there red with embarrassment and with one wet leg. They quickly settled their bill and practically ran out of the taverna to their car. It was now safe to release the laughter that had built up inside us to breaking point. Even the waitresses, who were righting the tables and chairs, allowed themselves a little snigger. Us? We were in tears!

Across the water, the orange glow of a city at night radiated from the Albanian coastal town of Sarande. Kassiopi was more sedate than of recent years. Nightlife was quieter, the tavernas emptier, the bars sober. We finished our drinks and wandered back over to the café bar we had used earlier in the day. Coffees were bought and pleasant conversation was exchanged once again with Steve. It was only 10.30 but a mixture of laughter, drink, food and warm night air began to take their toll on our not so young bodies. So we thanked our host, bade our goodbyes and headed off up to the taxi rank. Once there, there were no taxis but a number to ring. I duly rang the number.

"Yes?" A woman's voice asked.

"Hi. Could I have a taxi please from Kassiopi to Kalami?"

"Are there no taxis there?"

Would I be ringing if there were? I thought to myself but refrained from actually saying so.

"No!" I replied

"Well, they're all at the airport then." she sounded surprised that I didn't know that.

"So how long before they're due back?" I asked, half knowing the answer.

"I've no idea?" came the curt reply.

There was nothing for it, so we wandered back to the bar.

"You are back my friends?" asked Steve.

"Yes." I said. "There are no taxis at the rank and they don't know when they'll be back."

"There should be plenty of taxis?" he said, with a hint of confusion in his voice. "Leave it with me and I'll ring round for you!"

And off he went. Ten minutes later he returned.

"I don't understand it? I've rung round everywhere and can't get you a taxi!"

We all looked at each other and said "What the hell do we do now?"

"Leave it with me my friends." said Steve, and disappeared again.

Five minutes later he returned and stated that he'd just got his friend out of bed and he was going to run us back. We sat, mouths open, not knowing what to say. Thank you didn't seem enough. Sure enough, two minutes later an estate pulled up outside and he beckoned us to climb inside. We shook Steve's hand till his arm nearly fell off, thanked him profusely and said we'd be back to see him before we went home.

The journey back was a quiet one as the driver didn't speak any English. Some 15 minutes later saw us dropped off right outside the reception of our apartments. I handed the driver €20, we all shook his hand, and I repeated efharisto many times. When he'd gone we all agreed that had this happened back in England the restaurant owner would have probably just shrugged his shoulders at our predicament and did nothing, such is the friendliness of the Greeks. We retired to our respective rooms stunned at this act of kindness.

The next morning I returned to Kassiopi. The main reason was to buy some antibiotics that are sold straight over the counter without prescription and are cheaper than back home. I dropped in to see, Steve.

"Kalimera, my friend!" he greeted me.

"Kalimera Steve!" I replied. "I just wanted to thank you again for last night, that was very kind, and please thank your friend for us. We were all a little embarrassed that you got him out of bed just to run us back."

"Think nothing of it," he replied, "he was glad to help. Oh, by the way?" he said, "He asked me to give you this." and pressed to €20 back into my hand.

For a few seconds I wondered what it was for, then it dawned on me.

"No, no!" I protested, "This is for his petrol. It would have cost us at least that for the taxi!"

"You keep it, my friend, he was just glad he could help."

I was totally flabbergasted. Dragged out of bed at 11 o'clock at night, having to drive a carload of tourists all the way back to Kalami and he didn't even want paying for it! No matter what I said he wouldn't take the money, so I thanked him again and left to catch the next bus back.

The generosity of the Greek people is often spoken about. Here, I'd just witnessed it firsthand.

As the holiday drew to a close so the reality of returning to the real world began to sink in. Relaxation would be replaced by rat race; tranquillity by time clocks; amity by aggression; paradise by platitude. A week in Kalami is never enough; it felt like we had stepped off the plane only yesterday. A feeling we all shared. The ride back to the airport was taken in near silence so that every last vista, every last essence of the island could be absorbed into our very being, etched onto our brains through sight, sound and smell. Every mile ridden was a mile closer to where we didn't want to be.

"One day we'll come back here permanently," I said to Julie, reading her thoughts.

"Chance would be a fine thing?" she added.

I squeezed her hand as we pulled into the airport

Chapter 9

Dolphins for Dinner

Oh, how we'd longed for this holiday! Not just because it had been a year since our last sojourn to Kalami but because we'd spent a miserable two weeks in May of this year on the Canarian island of La Palma. Having looked at dozens and dozens of alternatives, from Albania to Turkey; Egypt to Crete; France to Sardinia; our patience was wearing pretty thin and the alternatives exhausted when we chanced upon the exotically named Hacienda San Jorge. We've always liked Gran Canaria so decided, after much searching on the web for something different; to try somewhere that nobody that we know of had been before. The write-ups of the aparthotel were excellent; the stunning photos of the rooms and grounds likewise.

"It's within our budget?" I said to Julie.

"Go ahead and book it then! " she said, "We can't seem to find anything else"

We always go self-catering and always ask for a sea view where ever we go as we like to sit in the evening on our balcony, sipping a glass of wine and watching ships pass in the night.

The hotel didn't disappoint. Reception was a huge marble affair replete with palm trees, leather settees and a full-size piano. A large glass atrium ran along one side which served as the bar. The walk to our room through the grounds was as impressive as the pictures we'd perused. Palms of all types from all around the world festooned the grounds, along with brightly coloured parrots and cockatoos. The large swimming pool was fed from a waterfall. The apartment itself was spacious and airy and indeed did have a sea view, or would have if they were to cut down the two huge palm trees growing right outside our balcony. They did eventually move us but they needn't have bothered as no ships ever seemed to go past the island!

The following morning, we ventured down to the beach where we lay on black, volcanic sand. We knew about this before we went but what we hadn't expected was the bay to be surrounded by black volcanic rock as well. Add to this the fact that the man-made wave breaks that they had positioned a couple of hundred yards out at sea were actually black, octagonal concrete blocks! We lay there in the morning sun trying not to think of our bleak surroundings. Then, at about 11 o'clock, black clouds suddenly appeared from the mountains behind us and stayed there for the rest of the day! This was not a one-off for this happened every single day while we were there, so-much-so that you could practically set your watch by them. A few times we would venture back to the hotel to lay around the pool only to be attacked by flies and ignored by the other guests.

The evenings were also a dead loss. A group of about ten restaurants huddled together three stories high en bloc. Only one played music, the others were devoid of any atmosphere whatsoever and quite often we were the only ones in them even though they displayed 'reserved' notices on most of the other tables?

We soon came to realise that out of all the patrons staying at the hotel only four of us were English, all the others were German, hence the reason we were ignored. This was borne out by the information books in the reception. Out of 37 folders extolling the delights of La Palma, only one was in English and there was no information in it anyway! Try as we might to make friends we were looked down upon by the rest of the guests, some sneeringly so. Eventually, just for something to do, we would walk into the main port of Santa Cruz some 50 minutes away. To do this meant climbing

90 odd steps up to the main road which would then take you past the islands main army barracks where a shooting range was in constant use. As we actually did this for 12 days out of the 14 we were there, we were convinced the guards on the main gate probably thought we were spies, gathering information on troop movements and base layout.

Once passed, we would then have to walk down through the industrial area, which included a petrol refinery operating 24/7. Santa Cruz itself rigorously observed siesta time so by 2 pm everything, including cafés, was shut until after 5. We were surprised to see an English liner docked one day, (it must have snuck in at night!) We also found it laughable that waiting on the dockside were a hoard of coaches, not to take the passengers on some island tour, but to pick them up and deposit them at the dock gates some 200yds away! By the time they queued for the coaches, it would have been quicker to walk to the gates! So disappointed were we by the holiday that by the third day we both wanted to go home, and we still had eleven days to go!

When we did finally get back to dear old Blighty, we immediately got on the web, booked one week in Kalami for September AND two weeks for the following May!

So, we were back. Back where we belonged. Back to our home away from home. Back to our little bit of paradise. Back to where we were among friends we hadn't even met yet.

We had emailed Gina at the A&A apartments before we came away requesting a high floor room with balcony so that in the evenings we could watch the distant, warm glow of Corfu Town and the comings and goings of the ferries and liners. She didn't disappoint.

As was customary, our first port of call on our way to the beach was Thomas's. Alexandra was there as usual, with a new daytime waiter. Her grin filled the taverna as she hugged and kissed us both. Her English had not improved any so our "Hello, how are you?" had to be kept too just that. She nodded, replied "good" and just kept on smiling. To save an embarrassing silence I immediately asked if we could book our usual table.

"Sixteen?" she asked to make sure.

"As always!" I replied. "7 pm?"

"OK!" and she wrote it in the book.

Conversation over and Anglo/Greek friendships rekindled. Ten seconds later we were lying prostrate on a couple of loungers. I took a deep breath, exhaled and let my mind and body sink into Kalami.

THWACK!

I raised my head up, intrigued by the strange sound but saw nothing.

THWACK!

There it is again!

THWACK!

"Can you hear that dear?" I asked Julie

THWACK!

"Yes. Where's it coming from?"

THWACK!

I looked behind me, then out at sea.

"I've no idea!" I replied

THWACK!

By this time I was propped up on my elbows, shading my eyes from the sun before finally tracking down the source of this odd noise. Just by the jetty, about 50 feet from where we lay, Thomas, who had obviously been out fishing, was busily splatting an octopus against a rock!

"Why do you think he's doing that?" asked Julie

"Maybe the fish out here fight back!" I proffered.

Before I could suggest an alternative answer Vlad, who had been standing behind us also intrigued by the noise said;

"It is to get the ink out of the squid!"

"Oh! Hi, Vlad" I said. "Didn't know you were there?"

"Yes, it gets the ink out and......." here he faulted for the right word, "Makes the fish easier to eat."

"More tender?" I offered

"Yes! More tender."

It seemed a brutal way to tenderise meat but perhaps the only way to extract the ink. Anyway, I didn't care what he did with it cos I didn't eat fish anyway. As long as he didn't tenderise my lamb the same way!

Some moments later our old canine companion, who we hadn't seen the last time we were here, sauntered up to renew friendships.

"Hello Ben!" we both greeted, "Haven't seen you for a while have we!"

"That's not Ben. Ben died!" said Vlad.

"But he looks the spit of Ben!" I said

"Is Billy." he replied, "Ben now gone."

And with that, he went back to setting up the tables and left us to make a new friend.

Our first meal was always the best. Perhaps because of the expectant and now familiar setting or because of the romanticised image we had fixated in our minds. Shirley Valentine's retsina by the water's edge paled into insignificance here. Here, there were no lagered up louts, no annoyingly loudmouthed diners who cared not if all and sundry were privy to their conversations and opinions. There were tables of two, three, four....up to groups of eight dining together. Yes, they talked, yes they laughed, yes they could at times be loud but there was nothing offensive about them. Their laughter and gaiety added to the warm ambience of the taverna and the balmy night air. It's as if Kalami forbade solemnity. Children were welcomed with the same geniality as their parents. Where kids running about in a restaurant back home would be frowned upon, here they were met with smiles and laughter.

Signs that hard times were hitting the Greek economy were evident on the arrival of the now familiar travelling musical quartet, they had now become a trio! One accordion; one guitar; but still the all-important tambourine/collection plate. And whereas the previous years had seen one visit per week, now it had grown to three. Times were indeed desperate.

Unfortunately, as good as they were, you were reluctant to pay three times to hear the same tunes every time.

The end of the meal always seemed to come too fast. Yes, we could have stayed and eaten dessert or drunk more wine but that would have deprived others of Thomas's hospitality, not to mention his excellent fare. Our pockets would have suffered too, as well as our waistlines! Hand in hand we ambled along the beach, breathed in the temperate salty air and stood and looked out across the dark waters.

I took a deep breath. The one you take when you feel at peace with the world. The one that exhales contentment.

"I don't believe it!" Exclaimed Julie the following day as she returned to her lounger. "That woman I was talking to in the sea, I used to go to school with her!"

"You're kidding?"

"No! We weren't in the same year but I remember her and she knew the same people as me. How spooky is that?"

"Well, they're always going on it being a small world, here's your proof," I said.

"I thought I recognised her. Didn't you see me talking to her for the past 45 minutes?"

"No, I must have dropped off." I lied.

I had wondered why she was taking so long to swim so I took a peek and saw her talking to another stranger. 'Oh no! Not more new friends!' I thought to myself and made out I hadn't seen her.

Julie then launched into a list of people that they both knew. Who was going out with whom; who was who's brother/sister; what became of so-and-so etc. Totally lost on me as I had no idea who these people were. The only surprising fact was that the actor Peter Davison and the footballer Ray Wilkins both attended that same school.

As was the norm now, our lunchtime repast was taken back at the apartment. A decision we began to regret for this year there seemed to be a profusion of wasps. As soon as we sat down to eat, they would appear from nowhere. We had not seen nor heard one solitary winged beasty since our arrival at Kalami, but the moment Julie placed our ham or cheese salad on our balcony table they would magically materialize like Pavlov's dogs!

Now, the most interesting, and annoying, thing about wasps is that over millions of years of evolution they have sussed man out. They have realised that when a human lashes out at their encroachment onto his food or into his territory, they always strike in a straight line. In other words, once the proposed strike is initiated it will carry on its intended path without deviation. Regardless whether it's the back of the hand swipe, or the newspaper smash, or the open-handed swat – to be effective it must make contact in its linear trajectory. If the said strike was to have to change direction on its travel to the offending stinger there would be less power on making contact. On the other hand man, over those same millions of years, has failed to recognise this minor but all important fact. But the lowly wasp has taken all this in and uses it to their advantage. Working in groups of two, three or four, they would assault from various angles to cause maximum disorder. The result was a mad and confused series of mid-air flailing of arms like two demented tic-tac men. Occasionally a yelp would go up but this was only because we'd managed to connect with each other rather than our intended targets, who were missed time and time again as they performed a perfectly executed series of dodging manoeuvres. They had perfected the art of hovering in one place just long enough for you to get a fix on them, like a fighter pilot zeroing in on his target with laser-guided missiles, and then moving at the last split second as the button was pushed.

    When the last attacker had been shooed away or beaten into submission the table looked like the Somme. Food had been redistributed round the plate, condiments lay where they had fallen, cutlery was scattered to the four corners. Defeated, we fell back behind the safety of the patio doors to relish what was left of our rations, tend our bruised and battered limbs and return once more to the beachhead, broken and demoralised. Tomorrow we would regroup and try again.

    Exhausted from the war of the wasps we took up our places once again on our loungers. I was just settling into an afternoon of quietude and contemplation when a voice that sounded like a cross between John Hurt and Jeremy Clarkson piped up from a table just behind us. It belonged to a man that, as we found out from his loud and alcohol-induced conversations, was with his wife, nanny and five-year-old son. One of his most annoying habits, apart from just speaking, was to keep saying "Oi, Oi, Saveloy!" to his son every ten minutes with his deep, posh, nasally accent. He had one of those voices that was hard to quieten down. It was naturally loud and he made full use of it. We learnt that they were renting a private villa just of the main road (don't know where?), that his 'bloody wife' was useless (not sure about that?), that the nanny was overweight (definitely true!), that he was there to relax and drink copious amounts of alcohol (very true!!), and that he didn't care about other people's opinions (very, very true!!!). We hoped that he was going to vary his choice of tavernas so that we didn't have to suffer his grating voice and opinions every day and night. Thankfully, he did.

We were returning from our second favourite destination, Kassiopi. We had coffee'd with Steve, basked by the briny and were now travelling back. As we had caught the last bus it was unusually full. A mixture of Greek locals, school kids and tourists.

We shuffled down the aisle, eyeing a spare seat towards the back of the coach occupied by a shopping bag next to an old Greek lady who pretended to be asleep. Every now and again you could just see her eyelids flicker as she peeked out through the merest of slits to see if we were still there. We were. Then, unbelievably, a teenage Greek boy sitting with his noisy mates on the back seats just behind her noticed the spare seat and our standing, prodded her and, pointing to Julie, let loose at her in words that we're glad we didn't understand and probably wouldn't want to, thus resulting in her begrudgingly moving her bag and swapping seats. She never once argued or protested with the youth, obviously knowing she was in the wrong. I nodded to the youth in gratitude. Fortunately, she disembarked some four stops later and I was able to sit myself.

As is the custom on Greek buses, they still have a separate conductor who collects the fares. Once moving he wended his way along the coach, bracing himself against the seats as it bumped and swayed with the road, until he came to an English couple sat two rows in front.

"Two to Corfu town." asked the man.

"€4.20 each." said the conductor.

"But it was only €3.80 each when we came from Gorvia!" exclaimed the man indignantly. "That means we were overcharged!"

"But you go back Corfu Town?" stated the conductor in his broken English, "Is €4.20"

"Listen." said the not too bright Brit. "We only paid €3.80 each this morning so that's all we're paying now and we want a refund on what we were overcharged!"

"No, you go Corfu Town now, is more?" he tried again.

"Well it shouldn't be more!" his wife threw in "We only went to Kassiopi and now we're going back!"

The conductor opened his mouth to try again, shrugged his shoulders and, realising he was onto a loser with these halfwits, charged them the lower fare AND gave them a refund. The pair looked very pleased with themselves for saving what amounted to about 30p each. What they couldn't seem to grasp, but everybody else could, was that the reason the fare was cheaper is that Gorvia is a few stops outside Corfu Town, thus it's a shorter journey and hence a cheaper price! While they both sat there self-satisfied we all sat quietly laughing at them.

We woke to an anomaly this morning. Clouds! Not just ordinary clouds though. Dark, drizzly ones. We were unused to this and were at a loss at what to do. We had already visited Kassiopi and we knew Corfu Town better than our own village. We elected to wander down to Thomas's for a coffee and hoped it was a passing folly.

Two hours and several cups of coffee later we realised this wasn't going to pass. We could have stayed in the taverna but that would have been costly, both in our wallets and our waistlines. Begrudgingly we hauled our towels and costumes and lotions back up to our apartment, sat on the balcony and crosworded ourselves into submission.

Lunch came and went; so did umpteen Sudoku's, quiz words, spot-the-differences, word-searches and code breakers, but still the clouds and the drizzle persisted. It wasn't cold by any stretch of the imagination but the overcast, damp skies made it feel so.

We continually scanned the horizon for any sign of a break. There were, but they were far off over the Albanian mainland. By all accounts, we'd been fortunate. A couple of times in the past we'd been told on arrival; "Lucky you weren't here last week, practically rained every day!" But like I was fond of saying, annoyingly so sometimes; "You can't have a rainbow without the rain!"

It was around five before the clouds began to thin. Too late now for the beach; too early for Thomas's.

"Why don't we stroll round to Kouloura, have a coffee, sit for a while then walk back round" suggested Julie.

"Might as well!" I replied, "Better than sitting around here for another couple of hours."

We got ourselves ready and climbed the steps up to the main road. The clouds had broken fully now and the orange glow of the setting sun reflected off the lofty mountains of Albania making them appear as if covered in autumn leaves. It had warmed up too. Gone was the chill of the dampness and back was the solace of the afternoon sun. We strolled slowly down the gradual incline looking over hedges and fences at the handful of private villas hugging the hillside, their views uninterrupted across the blue ocean and the Albanian coastline. A couple even had horizon pools where it must have felt like you could swim over the edge and straight into the Ionian.

We grabbed a table by the harbour wall and ordered coffees. Apart from another couple, we were the only other patrons enjoying the early evening tranquillity. Below us, a fisherman readied his nets for the nights foraging. Crammed in the small harbour were a mixture of pleasure craft and fishing boats, so tightly packed they all moved as one with the ebb and flow of the tide. As we sat looking northwards a long, black, sleek motor yacht slowly inched its way round the headland heading south to who knows where. We watched in awe as it glided silently, effortlessly, through the water, hardly causing a ripple on the surface. Then, magically, two dolphins appeared, one to the front and one to the side of the vessel as if guiding it to its destination. So similar was its shape to that of the dolphins that we wondered if they had mistaken it for one of their own.

We sat for what felt like an age, silent, as it sailed past and out of sight. Once gone, voices began to be heard again and the busying of waiters resumed. Only then were there murmurings of envy, envy rather than jealousy.

It was an unhurried stroll back round to Kalami. To our right, a number of villas peppered the hill; to our left, a handful clung to the rocks as they swept down to meet the sea. The ones to our right sat high up and were gained by steep driveways, their gardens kept back by high walls of local rock draped in plumbago and bougainvillaea. To the left, we looked down mostly on to the roofs of these properties.

We had intended to visit our usual haunt but decided on the way back to dine at the White House instead. To save the embarrassment of having to walk past Thomas's without actually entering we kept to the road that ran behind his taverna. We knew we weren't beholding to him but we felt a little disloyal by choosing somewhere else to eat, and we felt that if he didn't see us then it wasn't so bad.

We were fortunate to get a table that sat alongside the small jetty attached to the taverna. It was that quiet time, just before dusk, where the cooling air gave rise to an echoing ambience. Keep nets and lobster pots tied to the jetty hung in the clear waters displaying their catch for those wanting fresh fish. It felt strange looking back across at Thomas's, it was a perspective new to us. Suddenly, without so much as a hint, a speedboat rounded the headland to our right, aiming straight for the middle of the bay. Behind it a steel cable towed a lone skier, coursing and turning, repeatedly cutting back and forth across the wake of the craft spewing a plume of water into the air behind him. He held the attention of all that watched as he twisted and turned and flipped before finally losing his grip and disappearing below the waters. There was a stifled cheer as this happened although I'm not sure if this for his mastery of his art or his sudden demise! The boat did a U-turn, drew up alongside the wading skier, handed him the tow rope and off they went back from whence they came never to be seen again.

In the now dusk light we bathed in the glow of the oil lamp that sat in the centre of our table.

The millpond still waters of the bay lay like a darkened mirror. The white mast lights of the three yachts anchored in the bay glowed their warning. But there was still just enough of the evening light to illuminate two dark figures breaking the surface of the water, disappearing as quickly as they had materialised. A few seconds later, they emerged again, this time closer to our jetty. But this time the two dolphins hesitated a little longer before diving again. We weren't sure if they were the two we'd seen earlier or another pair but it didn't matter. As they surfaced for a third time, a little further out, they swam around for a while as if checking out the bay, their shiny black skins reflecting the lights of the tavernas. Just as silently as they arrived, they disappeared again. The next time we spotted them they were two small dots far out at sea.

Alas, all good things must come to an end as they say and today was the penultimate day before our departure from this, our little piece of heaven. We lay all day without mentioning it, hoping if we didn't then it wouldn't be true. And, as it was our last night, we knew there was only one place to spend it. We made straight for table 16 where a lit candle, a flowered vase and a 'reserved' sign awaited us. We were in no hurry to order, telling the waiter that we hadn't made our mind up every time he came to us. We just sat in silence; sipping our wine and gazing out at the vista so that it became indelibly imprinted in our minds, to be called up every time we felt down or fed up with the British weather. Even after finishing our meal and our wine, we still couldn't pull ourselves away and sat for what seemed an age before accepting the inevitable.

As if on cue, as if to remind us of what we'll be missing, a huge, white, vividly illuminated liner slowly hove in to view as it ferried it's cargo of spent vacationers back to port in preparation to disembark its passengers unhappy, like us, that their holiday was at an end, and await the arrival of those full of good cheer that theirs was just about to begin. It seemed to take forever to cross the headlands of the bay, but we didn't care, it *could* take forever as far as we were concerned. As it glided serenely across the now dark waters its ghostly reflection mirrored its journey.

We still felt like we owed Thomas and Alexandra a return gift for the presents they gave us some years earlier but were at a loss as to what was appropriate. Julie suggested a souvenir of the royal wedding that had taken place this year between William and Kate. To my mind all that was on offer was tacky. And, would they be interested in having a souvenir of British royals? No, I wanted something that was English but didn't have a union jack emblazoned all over it or a picture of London or a Beefeater etc. Fortunately, we were shopping in Chelmsford one Saturday which just happened to be staging a farmers market. 'Ideal!' I thought, 'there must be something here that's decidedly British?' The usual things were on offer. Cheeses? (Wouldn't travel very well). A plant? (Dead before we get there). Handmade crafts? (Most of it tacky). We were running out of options when we came across a stall selling flavoured English vinegar. Eureka! Thomas loved his food and I thought this would be a great way of experimenting with cooking.

"This will make a great present for them as I don't think they have flavoured vinegar in Corfu!" I said.

On hearing this the young guy with the stall asked;

"Whereabouts in Corfu are you going?"

"Kalami!" I replied. "Do you know of it?"

"Know of it?" he said, "I learnt to scuba dive there!"

"You're kidding!" Julie and I said in unison.

"No, my mum owns a place in Kassiopi, I often go there."

This world of ours is definitely getting smaller.

We handed it to Thomas as we went to say our goodbyes. At first, he looked a little puzzled.

"It's flavoured vinegar," I told him

"Yes, yes!" he said in a thankful but mystified way.

"This one is apple and this is raspberry flavoured. You can add them to your cooking or just pour them into a dish and dip bread in them."

"Ah, thank you, thank you," he replied.

"They were made not too far from where we live," I said.

"You make this yourselves?" he asked

"No. No! They are made near where we live."

"Ah!" he understood now. "Please, I go get Alexandra and we find gift for you!"

"No! We don't want anything in return. This is for your friendship, hospitality and good food."

He embraced us as if we had just given him the crown jewels.

"We're back for two weeks next year Thomas so see you then.

"Goodbye my friends!" he said with a smile as warm as the sun.

Unfortunately, Vlad was not working that evening, which was a shame as we wanted to give him a good tip. All the tips the waiters are given all go into one pot to be shared, but we wanted Vlad to have ours personally and keep it for himself. Without him there we couldn't really give it to

Thomas to pass on as it would have gone straight into the pot.

"We'll make up for it when we see him next year," said Julie.

"Yeah," I said. "Only eight months to go!"

Addendum

On our most recent visit to Kalami (2015), there have been a few changes which I feel need a mention to save confusion.

Firstly: The Asonitis and Adonis (A&A) apartments are now known as the San Antonio Hotel. They are in the throes of being refurbished but the self-catering option no longer exists. Instead, it is B&B, half and full-board. It also now has its own beach bar with a decked seating area.

Secondly: The entertainment at the Cocktails and Dreams bar now consists of the Greek dancing night and themed nights.

Thirdly: All three tavernas now have their own jetties.

Fourthly: The local buses now run a little later in the evenings.

Although time will tell as to whether the changes made are to the good or detriment of the bay one thing is for sure – Kalami is and will always be as beautiful as ever, for that will never change.

Dear reader.

I sincerely hope that you have enjoyed this book as much as I did writing it. I had no intention when we started visiting Kalami to ever write about it, it was just a suggestion made after my wife read an article during a rather dreary holiday in the Canaries, and so everything is solely from memory as no notes were ever made.

Whether you enjoyed it or not, I would very much appreciate it if you could leave a review on whichever site you purchased it from, i.e. Amazon, Kobo etc.

Thank you.

For more information about other books by the author, please visit:

www.davidjohn37.co.uk

Printed in Great Britain
by Amazon